MARY JANE WILD

TWO WALKS
& A RANT

MARY JANE WILD

TWO WALKS & A RANT

BROOKE WILLIAMS

HOMEBOUND PUBLICATIONS

Ensuring that the mainstream isn't the only stream.

HOMEBOUND PUBLICATIONS

WWW.HOMEBOUNDPUBLICATIONS.COM

Quantity sales. Special discounts are available on quantity purchases by corporations, associations, bookstores, and others. For details, contact the publisher or visit wholesalers such as Ingram or Baker & Taylor.

All Rights Reserved
Published in 2021 by Homebound Publications
Cover Design and Interior Design by Leslie M. Browning
Cover Image © Philip Graves
Image of Hermit Card © Gloria Sanchez
ISBN 978-1953340207
First Edition Trade Paperback

10 9 8 7 6 5 4 3 2 1

Look for our titles in paperback, ebook, and audiobook wherever books are sold. Wholesale offerings for retailers available through Ingram.

Homebound Publications, is committed to ecological stewardship. We greatly value the natural environment and invest in environmental conservation. For each book purchased in our online store we plant one tree.

DEDICATION

For the women in my life, all of you,
for your power, beauty, and patience.

The desert never
mentions arrival. Solar

heat, sky, dust—
light, a few parched
colors: they

rinse so far
through me
there's nowhere

else to go. I
set out.

—David Hinton, "Desert Poems"

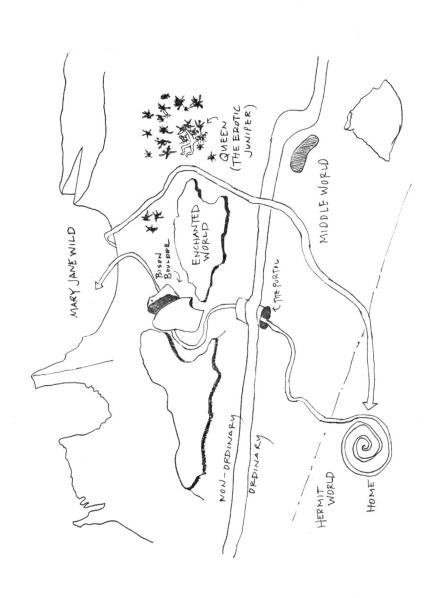

WALK ONE

NOVEMBER 10 - NOVEMBER 13, 2016

TUESDAY, NOVEMBER 8ᵀᴴ, **2016,** was the end of one thing and the beginning of something else. Donald Trump had been elected President of the United States.

Wednesday, to avoid thinking about the implications of the election, I cleaned out a storeroom I'd been unwilling to face for years. A pack rat had moved in and based on the contents of its nest, it had been living there for a while. I'd seen the chaotic nests of *Bushy-tailed Wood Rat (Neotoma cinerea)* in many wild canyons. This one, constructed of prickly pear cactus, but also small tools, sprinkler spare parts, coins, pens, insulation, and paper clips, demanded my respect.

Thursday, I loaded my pack and walked out the back door. Besides what I needed to sleep (no tent, no storms forecasted), I had two Tasty Bite meals, four hardboiled eggs, two packets of instant oatmeal, chicken soup, and three instant coffees. I had five bottles of various sizes filled with water—more than a gallon total. My map was in my chest pocket, with three pens and small black notebook.

With a hiking pole in each hand, I said 'goodbye' to Terry and walked out the back door. I hurried south into a gorge that runs around our house, protecting it from the unpredictable floods. I crossed the large field where early ranchers once grew alfalfa, and opened the pink gate separating private from public land. When I stepped through the opening as I'd done one hundred times before, I noticed the change. The trail along the old fence line I typically use to cross the valley had been replaced by a different, yet familiar path.

I'd followed Coyote along this route during numerous shamanic 'journeys' I'd taken while sitting trance-like in my study. I'd *chased* him along this trail, into a major arroyo, through the portal separating ordinary from non-ordinary reality, up an unnamed canyon, and into a cave at the base of a boulder. There we would sit at a large table and talk.

Until that moment, ordinary reality had been entirely separate from non-ordinary, or shamanic reality. For the first time, they blended together into a new, third reality.

With nothing in front of me but a sea of sage, I set out on Coyote's trail, a pair of ravens accompanying me. My old legs felt better and better as I moved through the desert, between cactus and sage, Castleton Tower a distant compass point. When I stopped to tighten my shoes, I didn't notice my three pens dropping out of my pocket into the red sand.

Lately, I'd been wondering how and why spending time in wild solitude creates a need in us—a need to contribute to the greater good beyond individual reward.[1] This is part of the story I've been exploring—that our modern lives have little in common with those we evolved to live, which may be the root of many of our problems. While this story moves side to side, its forward direction is constant. Wandering pathless ways in the desert, everything I need strapped to my back, is as close as most of us get to the life evolution prepared us for.

If I'd had a predetermined direction, it did not exist in my new reality. I was wandering, my path divergent and varied. The rhythm created by my alternating hiking poles and my steps put me in a familiar trance. Distance and destination no longer mattered.

Earlier gathering my gear in preparation for leaving, Terry said I was like a little kid, glowing with excitement. I guess I was. That excitement grew as I moved closer to the steep ridgeline dropping south away from Castleton Tower. I'd marked a map with the route I intended to take and left it with her. "If I'm not back by Saturday, you might call for a search," I'd said. Still, I was comfortable knowing that if I didn't return, I might be impossible to find.

I dropped down the steep bank into the arroyo, which I followed to the portal. During my shamanic journeys Coyote would glance back from inside the portal, to be sure I was still following. Inside, the thick air kept the essences on either side from mixing with one another. Taking a deep breath, I opened and hoped I would be conscious of any 'ground truths' that might come to me over the next few days.

I moved quickly, like water. My joints were smooth and my muscles warm. I was alert and eager as the thick solitude split open, allowing me in.

Fifty million years ago, when a massive salt dome collapsed far beneath the landscape east of what is now Moab, Utah, the surface dropped hundreds of feet. Today, 300 people live in the bottom surrounded by the high edges of spectacular

Wingate Sandstone cliffs, dark canyons, and the iconic spires of the Castleton Tower climbing area. The Bureau of Land Management (BLM) has identified much of the landscape surrounding Castle Valley as having wilderness qualities.[2]

The most important aspect of my life to date, not counting Terry, my dogs and family, etc., is the time I've spent alone in wild solitude. Countless hours running in the Wasatch, the Foothills above Salt Lake City. Long climbs on skis, the rhythm is creating some magic hypnotic effect. Days and days wandering the desert.

I recognized that same familiar feeling as I moved up the drainage. I noticed the pulsing I often experience in Castle Valley. Was I feeling it? Or hearing it? I can never tell.

Coyote's Cave is a small dark opening at the base of a house-sized boulder. That small cave triggered a long stream of memories. Before I followed Coyote there, I'd walked past it a dozen times, never paying much attention. This time I remembered the break in my conscious mind the first time I visited it.

No one had been in the cave for a while. Coyote grabbed a broom and immediately began sweeping. Oil-wall mounted lamps lit up the room. A large wooden table was off to the left, covered with dirt and mouse droppings. Coyote brushed off the table, tilted it back, and laid it down on its side. Beneath it were three large ammo-cans, which he brushed off. One was green, one blue, and one yellow. Then Coyote told me the story of the Spore.

Humans breathe in the Spore, which addles their brains causing changes in their behavior. This story was similar to one I'd heard years ago, about a mushroom growing in Africa, the Korup Rainforest. A particular ant is involved in the reproduction of this mushroom. These ants typically spend their lives foraging amid the leaves and grubs on the forest floor. The unlucky ones breathe in the spores of the mushroom, which float in the air. Once the spore (Spore) begins developing inside the ant's brain, the ant does something it's never done before: it climbs a stalk of tall grass. Reaching the top, it imbeds its pincers securing itself to the grass stalk. Hanging there, it dies. The spore continues to grow and develop, and soon, a small mushroom bursts from the dead ant's head. The mushroom bursts open, spreading a billion more spores into the air for other ants to breathe in.

Once inhaled, the Spore in Coyote's story also addles the brain, causing unusual and non-sensical behavior. Those who inhale the Spore climb toward the highest point and begin making decisions based solely on their own wealth and power, often with no regard for what is good and right and necessary for life on earth. "When you witness people in power behaving in ways unbecoming to life itself, you're seeing the Spore at work," Coyote told me. He continued.

After first appearing in Africa, our earliest ancestors moved north and began spreading out across the earth. Some stopped in the Middle East where the ground was fertile. Instead of hunting game, catching fish, and gathering wild plants, they discovered spores and seeds, and began growing their food. This did not happen overnight but only after a long period of trial and error, success and failure—experimenting with many different crops. One spore they planted sprouted mysteriously into an inedible mushroom. This mushroom grew and spread its seeds randomly across the land. Because one farmer was able to produce food for many and because they no longer needed to move seasonally following the movement of wild game and plants, the first fruits of civilization appeared.

What is less known is that people were breathing in the spores from the mysterious mushroom. For most, the Spore caused a seasonal cough accompanied by watering eyes and sleight fatigue. Some men, having absorbed the spore into their brains where it grew, stopped thinking rationally. They could no longer feel empathy. Controlled by the Spore, they cared only about their personal wealth and power. While many used the time freed up by farmers to create beauty and culture and everything necessary to compensate for this new way of life, Spore-affected men developed weapons of increasingly greater sophistication and effectiveness, anxious to protect their wealth and power.

"This gets weirder," Coyote said.

Spore-affected men could be seen standing on cliffs on what was then the edge of the world looking out across the vast and endless sea. The Spore made them anxious with wanderlust, made them want to sail off toward the horizon, gambling that the world was not flat.

Columbus, the Spore thriving in his brain, was one of the early leavers. He took the Spore with him. Spores traveled throughout the world in the brains of sailors and explorers. The Spore thrived, wherever Europeans landed.

America was fertile ground for the Spore, and it spread like fire across the land. In the 1950's Spore-brained white men with their weapons, their wealth, had reached the pinnacle they'd aspired to. World War II had ended. The American economy boomed. Spore-brained white men used their power and their money to relegate women to a lower status. People of color were seen only for their efforts to serve white men. Everything natural had value based only in the price it could bring on Spore-man's market. If the price was right, no land, no people were beyond the reach of the white invading colonizers. Everything was fine for white men. Until it wasn't.

The Spore in the brain of a white man makes any means justify the ends, which are more money and more power. More control.

"Enough for now," Coyote said.

As my teacher had instructed me to do, I handed Coyote a gift (a stone into which I'd drilled two eyes, turning it into a bear). In turn, Coyote gave me a white cloth bag and smiled. I soon discovered that he'd handed me a bag filled with his shit.

Just past the cave, I stopped, pulled out the map, and put it right back, remembering that it did not apply to my new reality. Without thinking, I turned south along the upper edge of a new drainage. To the east, long skirts of stone and sand dropped away from the vertical sides of a massive mesa.

I'd planned a meditative walk in a familiar landscape, not high adventure/exploration in brand new territory, let alone new reality. Knowing I had no choice I turned and dropped off the edge into the unknown.

Traversing the next mile took me an hour. I stumbled down a steep incline of soft dirt, following deer, who, I've learned are effective in finding their way in and out of canyons. I imagined that from space these tiny canyons must look like a circulatory system, as they fork and fork again. Gravity tugged on me as it had the water which formed the gulches, arroyos, and drainages. Like the animals whose tracks I followed, I tried to stay as high as possible. Going down with the flow promised to end badly—at impossible pour-offs in slot canyons.

I was being carried through the landscape on the back of some large soft thing with massive ancient paws. I floated beneath cliffs and between gigantic boulders and trees, which also floated, although more slowly.

Whenever I thought I was stuck and might need to turn back, I found an animal track to follow—deer, coyotes, the occasional bobcat. I needed to slow down, check myself and focus on the rules I have when wandering alone: don't do anything I can't reverse; no jumping; step in the middle of things, not on their edges.

I dropped into small, veined canyons four times, thinking that the tall, opposite side would be the last, and I would stand on top and see the world spread out flat before me. And each time, I saw more of the same, unending cuts and fractures as if some huge fist was rising from beneath, cracking the entire surface of the earth the moment before it breaks through, shattering the surrounding landscape into a million deep red pieces.

I found my way in and out of yet another gulch and sat sweating on a boulder in the sun, taking a drink of water. I worried about water—I'd seen none and wasn't carrying enough to last the time I'd planned on being out. I wondered if water would be a problem in my new reality. Eager to get moving in the day's last light, I turned once more toward the mesa and climbed higher onto one of its skirts.

Although the sun stayed strong, and since I had no destination I chose to stop and camp in the large beautiful opening I'd seen from above, beneath a mammoth juniper tree.

I set up my simple camp as the shadow line moved across it like a massive curtain, pushing and pressurizing the air in front of it. Without a hint of motion, the temperature dropped as if attached to gravity.

My pack was light in deference to my bad left knee but still included a small camp chair, which I unrolled and at the head of my sleeping bag, facing one of the mesa's long arms as it caught fire in the late sun. To the left of the chair, I spread out my tiny stove and cooking pot, water bottle, and food sack. On the right I placed the book I'd brought—*The Infatuations*, by Javier Marias—on top of my parka. I put on my hat and headlamp, which I would need in a few hours, and sat down. I pulled my notebook and reached for my pens, only to discover that they were gone. At first, I felt useless without them. I laid my blank notebook to my left on top of the small bag that could only contain Coyote shit.

I looked forward to cooking and eating but waited for the sun to go down.

Donald Trump had just been elected President of the United States. I knew that a long walk was the best way to deal with the angst I felt. How could America elect a man whose main success was as a two-bit celebrity, who, based on everything he said during the campaign, has disdain for anyone not white, male, or rich. A man who unabashedly promised to cater only to those embodying the most radically conservative principles. My angst multiplied with my vision of drooling Utah white men—many of them close relatives—thinking finally, they would have everything the liberals have denied them. They would have the freedom to develop the wild places, to pollute the air and water, and to wave their guns around in public. To treat "other" as the means to their ends. They now have the stage to openly flaunt their supremacy. But, what really haunted me into leaving home to go wandering was ignorance: mine, as in 'ignore'—ance. As so many of us had done, I'd ignored the angry white racist male American. I'd assumed that he'd disappeared into history when in fact, he had been alive and smoldering beneath the surface of our lives.

No sound makes its own sound. Silence in the wilds is not an absence, but a presence. I made mental notes about the different qualities of silence—thrumming replaced by vibrations drowned by what can only be described as buzzing. But no sound until raven's wings slashed through the compressed light. No movement until a small, thumb-nail-sized, beige moth landed on my left shoulder. I alternated my view between that insect and my view of the vast and distant, reddening cliff face.

The moth sat there as long as I didn't move. It cleaned its antennae with its front legs, wiped its eyes, and flexed its wings. Did it know it would die soon? What is the lifespan of a moth? I wondered if, out there in the scientific world, someone knew this creature, its habits, its life-cycle. Does anyone know its name? I caught myself comparing my non-descript moth to those in Emmet Gowin's photos from South America—all the colors and patterns, each one an art project. I remembered that with any wild organism, what is "beautiful" or "plain" or "ugly" is that creature adapting, surviving.

The tiny moth, I thought, was a real and important element of lifeforce. As was I, moving across the rugged and real landscape. Lifeforce constantly moves into the future. It may be lifeforce that is the energy behind the spinning of planets around the sun, the movement of stars. Lifeforce is evolution, and evolution is lifeforce. Lifeforce is non-hierarchical—the tiny moth-like creature is no less important than a bull elk, or a dinosaur, or an aging man finding a way across the wilderness. Perhaps this one question rises above all others: does how I live my life support and free the force of other life, or does it diminish it, weigh it down, extinguish it?

The light-colored moth was highly visible perched on my blue parka. I thought of college biology—the peppered moth. As I recalled, this story illustrates natural selection, as Darwin envisioned it. The peppered moth exists in two phases, light and dark. In pre-industrial England, white phased moths dominated because they were camouflaged against the white bark of trees where they rested during the day. Birds picked the dark ones off of the tree because they contrasted to the light tree bark. With the advent of the coal-fired Industrial Revolution, soot from manufacturing plants darkened the tree-bark, making them safe for the dark moths and dangerous for the white ones. In a very short period of time, the dark moths outnumbered the light ones.

If a small moth can be content, this one sitting on my shoulder was. Once it had groomed and fine-tuned its antennae, it rested. It flexed its mouthparts—it could have been chewing something small enough to be invisible. I was beginning to cramp and knew I had to move. I challenged myself to rise from my chair in such a smooth motion that the moth would not feel the need to fly off. In this new and intimate world, the moth and I had roles in one another's lives.

The colors in the cliff above me—a gigantic prow—had shifted through the full spectrum of orange and had started moving through the scale of reds as the sun continued dropping. I lit my stove and while the water boiled I got up to see what the last light of day was doing to my camp. It had turned the red soil around me purple. I wandered over to a small wash following the tracks of a small rodent—a deer mouse? Nothing moved. There were no sounds. (How the lowering light increases the air's density, which thickens the solitude is a mystery to me.) The increasing darkness may not be the light leaving, not an absence, but the presence of a soft and tangible blanket of stillness forming around the light before putting it out. Although a bit tired and sore, I blamed the dense silence for my slowness moving back to my camp.

"*This* is wilderness. This *is* *Wilderness*", I thought, settling back into my chair. I know the feeling, regardless of which reality I happen to be in. I've read the Wilderness Act. I know all the arguments for protecting it. I've listened to smart lawyers defend it in court and in front of congressional committees and in the pages of all America's newspapers and magazines. I've written for years about my exploration of why in this modern age, we need wilderness in our lives. And, I've thought endlessly about what Thoreau meant when he said, "In wildness is the preservation of the world." These are merely words, but as I've discovered while making words my vocation, they are not static but dynamic. Words live and their meaning can change over time, adapt. The poet, W.S. Merwin, once remarked that the classics should be re-examined each generation to bring new understanding to a changing context. Words are not the 'thing' they describe. Our job as writers is to bring words as close as possible to the 'thing' they represent.

Drenched in silence, cliff colors changing, the feeling I had shifted beyond the hope of finding words that would come anywhere near it. As if I brought a body filled with chemicals which, when exposed to catalytic wildness, reacted, forming a new, never seen element, one made only for that moment.

I recalled, rising from the depths of that silence, those colors, that although much of the landscape surrounding Castle Valley, has been designated as Wilderness Study Area (WSA)—land the Bureau of Land Management has determined to have wilderness qualities, it has not received official Wilderness Designation. For years, people who care about wildness have supported Congressional legislation for "America's Redrock Wilderness Bill," which would forever protect 8 million acres in southern Utah. Many different efforts have successfully protected portions of these unique wild lands in the past. Based on reliable information, not only can we not expect any land protection during the Trump administration, we may see him respond to the carbon industry and rural Utah leaders and reverse protections currently in place.

I folded into my chair, pulling my sleeping bag high over me. Tasty Bite meals are perfect for short trips. Pad Thai for the first night, I wiped down the bag before placing it carefully in the boiling water, which I could re-use in the morning. While it cooked, I got organized so I would know where everything was, even in the dark.

My mind wandered off from where I sat—purely alone, threatened by nothing, protected by everything. Solid. Framed by cliffs, side to side, by wild silence from above. I thought of Bears Ears, a huge wild chunk of land in San Juan County to the south. We held out hope that President Obama[3], in his last days, would proclaim it a National Monument. This after years of failed process, phony negotiations, and continued threat from carbon development. Already, inspired by all the publicity, people from all over the world had descended on this pure place, which was not ready for them.

I thought back to the moment Bears Ears came alive for me. I was sitting with Terry in our Castle Valley living room with a dozen University of Utah Environmental Humanities Graduate students. Jonah Yellowman, a Navajo holy man, was there with Gavin Noyes, the executive director of Utah Diné Bikéyah. It was the last day of *Art, Advocacy, and Landscape,* the class Terry developed and we led together each year addressing a current issue, hoping to discover new humanities-based solutions. "Greater Canyonlands" was the subject that year. We'd spent four weekends visiting the landscape in question while meeting with environmental leaders representing the different proposals for protecting the environmentally, scenically, and culturally important vastness around Canyonlands National Park. Jonah and Gavin were the last to meet with the students. They presented the Indigenous proposal and called it "Bears Ears." This was the first time I heard the words.

Having wandered the canyons and mesas of the area for years, I favored the proposal co-generated by the Southern Utah Wilderness Alliance (SUWA) and the Grand Canyon Trust, which offered the most protection to the greatest area. Plus, I'd worked for SUWA and had been involved in the analysis and field work that led to their proposal. At a Washington D.C.

strategy meeting with the Department of Interior, we'd been told that while a new monument in southern Utah was on their radar, they wouldn't move on it until the different factions of the local environmental community were all on the same page.

The class was waiting patiently for Jonah and Gavin's arrival. Light rain began falling when we all went out on the porch to greet them. As Jonah entered our home, coyotes called in the distance. We all turned toward the desert dog's songs. I'd never heard coyotes singing in daylight.

We gathered inside and sat in chairs and on couches forming a circle around our living room. After introductions, Jonah blessed our home and everyone in it, first in Navajo and then in English. Terry turned to Gavin to share his perceptions of the Bear's Ears Campaign with the group. Although Anglo, Gavin has always had an alliance with Native people. He'd created and implemented a project designed to gather Indigenous knowledge about the Colorado Plateau. Conservation efforts had been drastically deficient in Native Voices, and Gavin's efforts resulted in the formation of a new organization representing the varied and diverse Native voices in all matters. In the Navajo language, "Diné Bikéyah" means "the sacred lands of the people."

Although I'd read it before, something shifted deep inside me when Gavin told our group that Diné Bikéyah's mission is to "preserve and protect the cultural and natural resources of ancestral Native American lands to benefit and bring healing to people and the Earth." What struck me was "bring healing to people and the Earth." For the first time, "People," meant *all people*, not just Indian People. I felt this idea sinking deeper into my body and settling as Gavin and Jonah described specifics using many-colored maps. That their proposal didn't cover as much acreage as the others no longer mattered. It manifested a deeper vision.

It was Jonah's turn to speak. Just then, those facing the eastern windows gasped. A rainbow appeared, but this one was different. Rather than arching traditionally up into the sky and down again, this one stretched horizontally across the tops of the distant formations, connecting them, one to another. Jonah smiled. "The Twins are nearby," he said, referring to the Monster Slayer Born-of-the-Waters—part of the Dine' Creation Story. We all went outside. Terry asked Jonah if this was common. "No," he said.

He went on to tell of Bears Ears, two perfect buttes in the center of the Navajo world, the source of many stories since the beginning of time, the place where the bones of his ancestors are buried, where his great, great, great grandmother was born. The longer he talked, the deeper I sunk into my chair. The more comfortable I became. When Jonah referred to "Sacred land Protection," I realized that this was a term with which I had a history.

In my own Mormon upbringing, the "Sacred Grove" was where Joseph Smith received the vision inspiring him to create the Church of Jesus Christ of Latter-day Saints. I'd been through many stages since stepping away from my Mormon foundation. I grew up assuming that anything considered 'sacred' was of 'God', for religious purposes, the opposite of 'secular' or of the world, human-based. Wendell Berry, a true hero of mine, wrote, "There are no unsacred places. There are only sacred places and desecrated places."

As Jonah talked, I wondered to myself what the term actually means. For me, a 'sacred place' is the site of a story that is important to one's personal or cultural life. The ancestors of white Euro-Americans—my ancestors—disconnected their stories from their sacred places when they left them. When my European ancestors got here, they created economies based on 'desecrating' the sacred places of others.

There was something elemental in Jonah's voice that morning. Jonah did not come to convince anyone of anything. Only to tell his truth, which I sensed came up through him from some place deep in the land that raised him. He came with stories given to him by his ancestors. Nothing seductive in his voice, said, "I have something for you, something that you need." Nothing saying, "Now, let me tell you how to earn what I have for you." He simply came to visit and share what he knew.

A boy in the Mormon Church, I grew up hearing white men speak in what we came to call their "Priesthood Voice," which they used to control us, scare us into conformity, promise us incredible gifts, but only once we were dead.

As Jonah spoke, his eyes moved around the room meeting each of our eyes, and then beyond: above and between us, looking out as if the stories he was telling were appearing in his mind at the exact moment he needed them, fully formed, a landscape of traditional knowledge, appropriate to our discussion. His frame of reference transcended time and space as we knew it.

When he finished, deep quiet pressurized the room, and no one moved. No one said anything for a full minute until Anna spoke up. "Thank you, Jonah, for these stories." She said, "We feel that you've shared some very sacred knowledge...."

"It is time," Jonah said.

A collective chill ran through the room.

I struggled to the door and opened it, releasing the pressure, spreading the chill out across the desert. We milled around as if nothing had happened. Jonah said, "We must have scared the coyotes away". With many miles still to travel, Jonah and Gavin left. We had some final class business to take care of. We sat out on the porch in a circle.

We talked about how complex the challenge of weaving these different perspectives together into a cohesive whole, attracting broad support with an eye toward the long view.

"How about a dinner party," someone suggested.

"A difficult dinner party," Terry said, smiling. "I believe that the most complex problems are more likely solved once the different sides of the issue have broken bread together, around a large table."

Two weeks later and after adding both extenders to the dining room table, we had our home's largest party ever. Local representatives from SUWA, The Nature Conservancy, Friends of Cedar Mesa, and The Grand Canyon Trust were there, and the former superintendent of Canyonlands National Park. Jonah and Gavin came. The two San Juan County Commissioners we invited, did not. Anna, from class, a master chef, made the dinner her final class project (she got an 'A'), bringing lamb and vegetables, all locally sourced, plus cornbread from a family recipe.

We'd been clear that this would be a gathering rather than a meeting, a chance to stand clear of politics and remember how much we all care about our greater home.

Steer clear of politics we did not, but due, I believe to wine and candles, we focused on details we all could agree on.

Later, Utah's environmental leaders concurred that the Diné Bikéyah proposal had the depth of cultural integrity lacking in the others. Not only would it be the most likely to succeed, but it told the deeper story of sacred lands, which is needed in the 21st Century. Although the dinner party may not have affected this outcome, a wider conversation began that night.

President Obama listened to the Bears Ears Intertribal Coalition (made up of people representing the Hopi, Diné, Zuni, Mountain Ute, and Ouray Ute tribes). He responded to the cultural values of the Bears Ears proposal, alongside the ecological, scenic, or wild values of the other allied groups.

It is time.

If the de-sacralization of Earth is even remotely responsible for these challenging and threatening times, then coming to an understanding of what "sacred land protection" means, is essential if we're to save ourselves and the life on which we depend. Indigenous leadership—in Utah with Bears Ears, but throughout the world—is moving us all forward into a graceful vision of the future.

A few days from full, the rising moon created a sleeping problem, but luckily I'd planned for it. I knew that the moon would be closer to the Earth than it had been for fifty years, a Super Moon. Sitting there, eating my meager meal, I bathed in the awe-infused moonlight.

I finished my pad Thai and then poured a few ounces of the still-steamy water into the measuring cup I used for a dish and stirred it with my finger, converting the Tasty Bite remnants into thin soup, which I drank knowing how precious water would become.

Clicking on my headlamp, I was sick about my missing pens. I always make notes, out of habit, or therapy, or addiction—as if until I write it down, nothing makes sense. I've learned not to wait for insights to force me to pull out pen and paper, but to pull out pen and paper and see what comes, one word and then the next. Pen-less, I was forced into the present, to watch and listen.

I pulled out my topo map, hoping for some sense of where I was, in my new reality. The map in no way represented the actual terrain I'd spent the previous four hours crossing. But then they rarely do. Maps are never the territory, but in these wild canyons, they are not even close. Topographers using aerial photographs of this area cannot hope to capture all the intrigue possible within forty-foot contours. I was on my own with no clue as to what I'd face in the morning. I had to trust, which was not easy.

I read in the light of my headlamp, cozy in giant down parka, nestled deep in its hood, a stocking cap and gloves, which I needed to remove to turn the pages.

Sleep stalked me. My familiar demons waited patiently while floating around my head. I could feel them, all four of them. They have names.

"TIP" ("Trump Is President"), the first demon, is shrill and uncouth and disrupts my silence with the reality that Trump is the president of the anything-but-United States of America. He embodies all that simmers beneath the surface of life: a fetid, long-stagnant, mixture of misogyny, racism, greed, and narcissism, which now stirred, rises from the swamp.

Demon Two, I call, "WHID" ("What Have I Done" with my Life?). This demon is single-minded. He asks over and over the rhetorical question, "And you, why have you wasted your one privileged life?" paraphrasing the grand poetess Mary Oliver's "And what will you do with your one wild and precious life?"

Demon Three casts doubt on my immediate physical situation. YATT ("You are Totally Toast) is always frantic. YATT is the alarm going off in my head, reminding me that I'm basically fucked. (Lost, thirsty, broken, or dead.) If not now, tomorrow, or surely the next day.

LISBB ("Life is still beautiful, but…."), the Fourth Demon, is a woman. I'm not sure how I know, but I feel her spirit. She enters my consciousness with impressions. I sense that she wants to help. She is clear. She reminds me that yes, much of what I've based my life on is unraveling, disintegrating, or dissolving. The elements of my foundation on which I stand, are disappearing. "Trust it," she says. "This can be a good thing."

TIP. WHID, YATT, LISBB.

Terry had given me a new parka a month before—an early Christmas present. This wasn't just any parka, but a Patagonia Fitz Roy down (made from *Traceable Down: 800-fill-power goose down from geese traced from parent farm to apparel factory to help ensure the birds that supply it are not force-fed or live-plucked*) parka. This parka is designed for serious alpine climbers—to wear during *"extended freezing belays"* or *"high-altitude emergency bivouacs."* Whether or not I deserve its protection, this parka had become my most prized possession.

I am anything but a serious alpine climber. I am, however, a committed wilderness explorer. You won't find photos of me in my new parka in a dogsled documenting bird migration across Antarctica. Or in shorts and sandals in a dugout canoe mapping a tributary of the Amazon River. Lately, much of the wilderness I explore is internal. This might have to do with my age (sixty-four) and my withering interest in the physical risks and the time commitment my previous obsessions with powder skiing, canyoneering, and climbing required.

While there are many ways into this inner wilderness, for me, the most effective access is through the "outer wilderness"—during a quiet, solitary walk in a familiar redrock canyon, or looking up through the universe on a moonless desert night, perched on a ridge watching a long view. Or sitting in a camp chair in the winter desert awed watching cliff light pass through a jagged prism of ice.

Awe may be the quickest, most direct route into that caldron of evolution we all have simmering deep inside us. We're taught to ignore it, this "id" that Freud thought needed to be contained if society were to function smoothly. This is the "core" biological human, that "secret person, undamaged..." in each of us, according to Human Ecologist Paul Shepard. Awe punctures any shell society has deposited over our true selves and, I believe, sparks evolution. I'd recently discovered the work of a Berkeley psychologist, Dachar Keltner, who has quantified the "pro-social" behavior associated with awe. According to Keltner, experiencing awe encourages us to contribute to the collective good of our species.

A stiff breeze moved past me, pushing the light ahead of it, darkness filling in behind it. I pulled up the heavy-duty zipper shielded beneath the down-filled tubes, sealing it against any cold. Over my hat, I pulled on the hood, specially designed to keep even the back of my neck warm. I was ready.

Paul Shepard said that the "mind expanded with the vista," referring to evolution and our ancestors' increasing brain size when they climbed down from the trees and wandered out onto the savannah. Anyone who has gazed out at an infinite view has experienced this expansion on an individual level. I felt it that evening: cliffs and sky no matter which way I turned. Thank goodness my hood was designed to cover a climbing helmet and therefore had room for my expanding mind.

Although the catalog description of my parka did not include the phrases, "for those deep winter days wandering aimlessly in the desert, or perched on a freezing ledge watching the long view, or perfect for extreme napping," it should have. Not only is my new parka perfect for what is fast becoming my preferred outdoor activity, having it encourages me to be out on the coldest, darkest days when staying inside might sink my mood.

With the sun gone and the last weak light suddenly consumed by blackness, I crawled into my sleeping bag.

No sound makes its own sound, I thought. Then I wondered if, like birds and insects and wildflowers, silence exists in many forms. Silence is not the absence of sound but the absence of distraction.

I woke up with all categories of negative thoughts flooding my brain, going a little crazy. As if TIP, WHID, YATT, and LISBB were all competing for my attention.

I cannot understand how Trump made sense to anyone this past election. So many go about their lives, upset because their team isn't winning, worried that they might miss the latest Fox News, or next *Apprentice* episode staring you know who. Or their next payment on their OHV (Off-Highway-Vehicle) on which they storm through the desert. Why can we not see that these are all part of the massive smokescreen designed for one thing: to keep us buying things that will keep our minds off of what's really going on? Why is "what is good for business?" a stronger question than "what is the meaning of life?" which, as I understand it, was once the universal question. How did we get here? What happened? The Spore must be piped into fast-food restaurants, through our televisions, and spread throughout Trump rallies.

I went down through the history as best as I could recall it, looking for clues, places in the timeframe where we should have known, and should have responded. Details. I felt as if I was fist fighting with Demon TIP ("Trump is President").

Trump had been around for a while.
We all knew who he was.
He flaunted his unearned wealth.
He falsely empowered men by seducing women.
He never apologized.
He went to all the parties (which his appearance
Downgraded).

Few took him seriously.

His class of white men had thrived for generations based on the color of their skin, their privilege, their weapons.

They believed that

—All other races were inferior to theirs; that

—All other genders were inferior to theirs; that

—All other species were inferior to theirs; that

—All other religions were inferior to theirs (theirs was the one and only god.)

—Their story was the best story. Their's was the only story that mattered.

They believed as they were told that they were the human race epitomized.

Doubt began creeping in.

—Other races began challenging them.

—Other genders began challenging them.

—Other species began challenging them.

—Other stories began challenging theirs.

Their power was being threatened. They got together to decide what could be done to ward off these potential challenges.

Change was the problem.

"Had change not occurred," they said, "America would still be great." "Let's make America Great Again," they said

"What?" they asked, "once made America great?"

—Other races knew their subservient roles

—Other genders knew theirs, too.

—Other species were means to white men's ends.

—The white man's story was the right story, only one worth telling.

How do we stop change? They asked.

'Change,' they were told, "is evolution."

—But we can't believe in evolution, they said.

—We need to stop it.

How do we stop evolution?

—Eliminating environmental policies in favor of business;

—Thwart creativity in young people by saddling them with student debt;

—Shrink national monuments;

—Encourage carbon development;

—Fight the protection of endangered wild species.

—Ignore the fact that there have been only two choices for three billion years: evolution or extinction. Eliminating evolution leads to extinction.

How to accomplish all this?

1. Angry white men need to stick together.

a. How do we do that?

    i. Say it's all about their money being taken from them.

    ii. Say it's all about their power being taken from them.

    iii. Say it's all about their guns being taken from them.

2. Elect Trump president. How do we do that?

a. Get the Christians to help.

    i. But Trump's values are not Christian values.

    ii. Tell them no more abortions.

b. Ask Russia to help

    i. Aren't they're our enemy?

    ii. Putin's also an angry white man who wants to keep all of his money.

c. Decide (control) who gets to vote and who doesn't.

In Utah, our politicians are hellbent on selling and destroying these public lands for the profit they seem to care more about than their own Mormon beliefs. They have, and those electing them have become so cut off from what really matters (nature, beauty, planetary health) —they have forgotten the importance of the future of life on earth.

Demon WHID ("What Have I Done" with my life?) took over, injecting a large dose of doubt. "What if," I thought, "what if all I've based my life on, all the knowledge I think I have, is wrong. What if none of the stories I tell are true. What if the republicans, the Mormons, and the Angry White Men are right? What if there really is a white-bearded male god sitting on a throne, and what if he did actually put white American men in charge? And what if climate change is a hoax perpetrated by Bernie Sanders, Al Gore, and Jane Fonda flying around in their black helicopters. Or it is real, but only for the rest of the world, and not us, the anointed/blessed ones? (Not here.) What if?"

Demon YATT ("You are Totally Toast") remained silent (thank god), having nothing to contribute. I said outloud, "Where are you when I need you, Demon LISBB "(Life is Still Beautiful, But")?"

This train of dangerous and painful thoughts came to a halt when I turned my head and looked at the moon. The wild silence was too powerful for demons. Wild silence neutralizes their power. Wild silence is an antidote to the Spore.

For months after learning about the Spore, I paid attention to the news and noted when I saw that the Spore had infected someone, altering their behavior, causing them to do something they'd never done before. Lying there in the moonlight, I recalled a thousand moments during the presidential campaign when someone said something that only made sense economically (it was part of their job to say such a thing) or politically. Trump's campaign manager, Kellyanne Conway, came to mind, talking about how Trump is not a racist, disavowing his support from White supremacist groups. "Conflict of interests? No way", she says. "His only interest is in Making America Great Again. Remember how much he's sacrificing to lead this country". Her demeanor and discomfort suggest that she doesn't believe what she's being paid to say, only in her 'alternative facts.' I wondered how far up the grass she has climbed and what her mushroom will look like when it bursts out of her head. Trump, hell, he inhaled the Spore ages ago. His entire adult life has been devoted to money; his brain power focused on financial gain regardless of the pain inflicted upon others in the process. Trump found the ultimate blade in the forest to climb up. The Spore continues to spread. I recalled an interview with a Trump supporter who, when asked all the questions floating around Trump, (his paying no taxes, his treatment of women, his racist comments, his, his, his,) said, "Irrelevant." Laying there on the firm ground, bathed in moonlight and thick silence, I knew that the poor man had taken a deep breath of Spore and it was already at work inside his brain.

I must have gone back to sleep because when I woke up to roll over on my stomach, the moon had moved across the sky.

WHID was waiting for me., The "What-Have-I-Done-" With-My-Life Demon always punishes me for all those years between books, all the unaccounted-for money, all the non-relationships with family. And more generally for being too timid and all those times choosing observation rather than action. He reminds me of all the times I've chosen the shadows and not the light. And that it's too late—I'm too old now to do anything about any of it. WHID would rather I just lay there and die, my rotting body becoming food for first coyotes, then ravens, then grubs. Fuck WHID. I'm used to him. I know him very well. He would soon grow impatient and leave me alone.

The Spore is everywhere now. We can't help but breathe it in. I turned toward the sky and breathed in the moon and felt the Spore shudder once, then wither. This is my work: making a case for wildness as the antidote to the Spore.

I let out a chuckle that rattled inside the hood of my sleeping bag, where I was hidden. Of course. Say that time spent surrounded by wildness is proportional to one's desire to contribute to the greater good. Then the opposite may also be true: one's propensity to focus on his/her individual wealth and stature while disregarding all other life forms, is *inversely* proportional to the time one spends in the wild world. Simply put: The Spore drives one toward wealth, and power, and status, which is killing the planet.

1. Wildness neutralizes the Spore, inspiring us to contribute to the greater good.
2. We evolved surrounded by wildness.
3. The Spore is a recent human phenomenon.
4. Unfortunately, the Spore is difficult to avoid in this modern world.

Since the Spore is good for business, it has become good for businesses to suppress, tame, and eliminate wildness, the spore's primary enemy.

Utah Congressman Rob Bishop's face filled my mind. He hates wildness. His actions on energy and climate are deplorable when considering the ability of humans to survive on this planet into the future. Much of his campaign 'war chest' comes from the carbon industry. Bishop's actions suggest that he didn't just breathe in the Spore accidentally but had it injected intravenously. In fact, he seems to be on a picc line that feeds him a constantly fresh supply.

Back to sleep for I don't know how long and then awake again with my head in the dirt—I'd slipped off of the pillow made of my parka in a stuff sack. The soft, subtle dawn light was just barely visible. The sharp moonlight had lost its power. Moonlight dissolves once the slight first light of dawn invades the black sky.

In choosing my campsite, I'd moved as far down the giant mesa's northwest flanks as possible, hoping for early morning sun. I waited in my warm cocoon. I would know the perfect time to get up. My bladder would tell me. In and out of sleep, remembering the dreaming but not the dreams, suddenly things got real. The least concealed of all the demons, YATT, the Third ("You Are Totally Toast") demon, began screaming at me. YATT had said to the other demons, "none of you were able to keep him awake doubting himself. Let me try." I was suddenly wide awake, assessing my water situation (which I'd done under much calmer conditions the night before.) I had only enough water to cook a meager breakfast, find my way in and out of I don't know how many more gulches, and without restocking, have little or no water left to use that night for cooking and drinking. Considering the heat I encountered the day before and was promised for the next, I panicked a bit. Potentially, I was "totally toast."

I relaxed once I remembered that the YATT demon was involved.

I dozed back into my sleeping back momentarily before the LISBB ("Life is Still Beautiful, But..."), the Fourth Demon shook me awake. I wasn't in the mood for her. She was relentless. She reminded me of my strong belief that *Wildness is access to our inner world, which contains the entire evolutionary history of our species, where we know how the planet might make the best use of us.* "Do you just think this is true?" she asked. "Or do you know it from experience?" She went on. "So how then, is the planet making the best use of you?" Regardless of whether she was being sarcastic, she struck a nerve deep and tender. Days later I would still reel from it, but like a kinked neck or a toothache I learned to accommodate it. I grew a different threshold of consciousness. I saw my place in life with a new realism, but the feeling was not what I would call ecstatic, more like a low-grade flu.

I'd created for myself the perfect situation for this aspect of wildness to act: absolute solitude, big wilderness. I never thought that by pulling away more and more layers, digging deeper and deeper into my inner world, that I might reach a point, a new frightening place that is deeper than I've ever been and scarier. Where nothing I see is familiar, and everything is age-old. But then, if I believe what I've spent most of my life trying to understand, I needed to take a hard look at it.

Or not. I've always spent significant energy questioning whether my efforts are worthy, if I'm contributing to the greater good, if my presence matters—is the air I breathe, the resources I consume, the space I take up wasted or not?

What if our ancient ancestors living their evolutionary lives didn't worry about any of this, only "what is that noise?" or "did that shadow move?" or "am I hungry?" Living the most meaningful life must result from living our most evolutionary, wild life, I rationalized. Perhaps, I thought, this is what Robert Thurman meant by 'coming alive' when he wrote, "Don't ask yourself what the world needs. Ask yourself what makes you **come alive**, and go do that, because what the world needs is people who have **come alive**."

My evolutionary life. Years ago, while traveling in England doing research on my ancestors, I read about Cheddar Man in the local newspaper. Cheddar Man is the name given to a skeleton discovered in the back of a cave in Cheddar, England (where cheddar cheese was first made) in 1906. At that time, archaeologists determined that based on the implements found with him these bones belonged to a primitive hunter. The article noted that the science of bones had advanced since Cheddar Man was first found, and recent analysis of his mitochondrial DNA determined him to be 10,000 years old. More astounding was the discovery that this DNA matched that of a school teacher currently living in the area. Being separated by 10,000 years is not enough time for significant biological changes to occur in modern bodies; Cheddar Man and the schoolteacher share the same evolutionary body, the entire evolutionary history of our species. I wondered if tested, I might find that I am another of Cheddar Man's descendants. Perhaps we all are. The discovery of a specific individual makes these ancient relationships real and personal. I believe that the inner world is our evolutionary self, which is more easily accessed and understood while moving around in wild places. Camped out in the wide desert, immense shadows shimmered on the distant cliff. Until then, my 'evolutionary self' appeared inviting and friendly but turned frightening the longer I was out, the closer I got.

I lit my stove to heat last night's water. I poured one instant oatmeal envelope (maple-flavored) into my cup. I figured that I'd eat the oatmeal first, then end with a cup of coffee which would clean the cup when I swirled the last few ounces before swallowing them.

As the water boiled, I poured a bit of it into my cup and mixed it with the oatmeal. Then I peeled one of four hard-boiled eggs I'd brought and cut it up into the oatmeal, something I'd never tried. It was wonderful! I cleaned out the cup as best I could with my spoon and poured in instant coffee and more hot water. Letting it sit a minute, I got up and pulled on my pants and shoes. Then I picked up my coffee and started moving around. I felt good. My legs felt loose and smooth and nothing hurt.

I wandered around, getting a sense of a larger circumference surrounding my camp, wondering which way to go. North was out of the question, a steep climb up one fold of the mesa's skirt, ending in an infinitely high, vertical wall. West, back the way I'd come, was my last choice. I walked northeast up a dry stream bed until it was too steep to negotiate and not spill my coffee. An easy climb took me to a high point from which I could see out. While this way seemed rugged and would no doubt present obstacles to negotiate, the vast labyrinthine expanse in the distance looked compelling. I wandered south, looking for a route more conducive to the resources I had available—water and energy. The sun lit up the cliffs in front of me. After walking five minutes, the landscape before me presented a clear way with no visible obstacles. South it would be.

Until I had a good solid plan for getting securely from Point A to Point B, YATT (You Are Totally Toast) took up all the space in my brain, leaving me no room for higher, expansive thoughts. Walking confidently back to camp, the Fourth Demon, LISBB drifted in.

Often, I forget what the demons tell me during those fretful, half-awake horizontal hours. I'm usually aware that the weight they give to issues is far greater than reality, not so with the last demon. LISBB (Life Is Still Beautiful...But) opened the door to a dark room I needed to walk through, as beyond it was something I needed, frightening though it was.

I gathered up my gear and packed it. I put on my pack and walked south leaving only footprints, which the next wind would obliterate.

Sure enough, ten minutes beyond the furthest point of my morning reconnaissance, I came to a cliff which, to negotiate might require breaking at least two of my rules: would I be able to reverse my route if later I came to an insurmountable obstacle?; and would I need to jump off a layer thicker than I could simply step from? Moving west a quarter-mile I found a deep canyon. Moving east, same thing. I followed the rim of the eastern gulch, willing to accept the worst-case scenario: that I would end up back at my camp with the only option to retrace my route from the day before. Still, I held onto hope for a break in the cliff that led to the bottom. I'd wandered the edge for fifteen minutes when my path crossed a well-worn animal path coming out of the gulch. I followed the tracks—deer or coyote or both?—to a foot-wide crack. The crack angled down across a vertical wall section ending at the top of a steep dirt slope. I stumbled down the loose dirt in a controlled fall, unwilling to consider the possibility that I might need to climb back out. The animals ahead kept me from wrong turns, dead ends, and in ten minutes, I stood firm on the water-hardened bottom of a major gulch.

My shoes were full of dirt so I stopped to empty them. I felt secure that I was now on a good route, to exactly where I didn't know. I sensed myself shrinking, being absorbed by the magic of this place. Having nothing but time, I sat for a while—the walls forming the gulch curved up over me, compressing the sky into a thin blue ribbon. I was inside a giant animal. Touching its rounded forms on the walls was visceral and alive, and I thought I detected a pulse.

I picked up my pack and started downstream. White alkaline powder and dry, cracking mud the thickness of eggshells covered the streambed, which hadn't been wet for weeks.

The vegetation changed as I neared the mouth of another small wash coming in from my right. The water trickling out of it formed a small orange stream where it had worn away the top white layer of mud, creating the opportunity for willows and low, yellowing grasses. The small stream working its way around a fist-sized rock had formed a small pool. Although alkaline powder coated the entire surface, this was the first water I'd seen, so I stopped to fill my empty bottles. Even filtered, the water I'd pumped looked like used bath water. While I might drink it only to keep from dying of thirst, making dinner with it would be no problem.

The wash made a long turn to the east, and a few human footprints appeared, suggesting I may be re-entering ordinary reality. The hard-grey surface changed to rich brown mud the moment I noticed the sound of moving water. The significant stream was lined with willows and tamarisk, and small cottonwoods had sprouted in places. Dark-eyed juncos flitted about in the willows, their tails flashing white. I followed the trail, hopping rock to rock as it crossed the stream six times in half a mile. When the stream took a big swing to the east, I turned north without thinking—up a tiny side canyon. Had it been formed by the scouring of boulders and branches from one angry flood or over ten thousand years of relentless seasonal flows?

I climbed the first pour off easily, knowing I could get back down it if I met the feared 'insurmountable obstacle.' With no consideration, I'd changed my plan. I relaxed, knowing I had the rest of one day and part of the next to wander aimlessly if I wanted. I was confident that somewhere west of me I'd find a route I could follow back home when the time was right.

Moving through the small canyon, walls merged and rose with the possibility of encountering a pour-off I couldn't climb. I struggled up a steep soft dune, at the top of which, hot and sweaty and with sore feet, I followed a perfect slickrock ridge for half-a-mile. I stopped in the shade of a large juniper tree, pulled my chair from my pack, and sat down. With nowhere to go and plenty of time to get there, I followed my thoughts as they wafted in and out of the washes I could see from my perch.

I pulled out my Marias book (Infatuations) and a hard-boiled egg and fired up my stove to boil the water I'd pumped from that alkali stream. "Trump," I thought. "He never gets out like this." Thinking back to the Spore and Trump's problem activated my anger and anxiety. Getting the root of a problem only works if that's the first step toward fixing it. Trump's Spore infection is everything I loathe and distrust about America. Too many modern Americans see only what Trump wants them to see—that he has mastered the economic system, which landed him on their television screens—which for many, is the basis of why they trust him, and one of the reasons I don't.

I'd inadvertently placed my pot off-center on the stove and it started to tilt. I grabbed for it but recoiled when I felt the heat. Helpless, I watched it fall, spilling its valuable contents, which were absorbed into the dry earth. With two quarts left, I wasn't in trouble, but what a stupid mistake. For the Fourth Demon, the timing was perfect. Life is Beautiful, But…

I reached into my shirt pocket for a non-existent pen. For fun, I looked all around and felt the breeze and noted all I would have missed had I been writing. In a way, writing stops the world. I can't be writing and being at the same time. Most of what I write about is being. The Fourth Demon could not have been suggesting that I not write. Or could she? *"Life is Beautiful AND look at all you've missed."*

For me, writing is art and art is creation, is embodied imagination, an end in itself, not a means to an end. When I've finished writing, I feel good about it—something warm and liquid-like flows in my chest. I feel the same moving freely out in the wilds: being. The two feelings—*being* out in the wilds and having written something good and original—must be related, two essences between which my life vibrates. And both similar to how the sun feels on my back and my face.

I sunk deeper into my chair. LISBB, The Fourth Demon, became more serious. *"Life is Beautiful, but …what if your 'One Story' is wrong?*

Long ago, Bill Kittredge, a mentor and friend, told me that his goal as a teacher was to help his students find the 'one story' they will tell over and over again the rest of their lives. At first, that sounded quite boring to me. But years later, I realized that that's exactly what I'd done. My one story is this:

We live in bodies that have not changed much since the Pleistocene. Many of our problems may be due to our living in a world vastly different from the one for which evolution designed us". This story has grown and changed, been added to and subtracted from. It has led me to believing that the length of the future is directly related to the length of the past we consider our own. If my past goes back 200,000 years to my early Pleistocene ancestors, then my future is also that long. This story gives me hope.

What if my story is wrong? My mood plummeted. Having the wrong story, a false story, a bad story seemed as good an explanation for many of my questions, as any. My story is antithetical to the American story, the most current version starring Trump. The millions of Americans who believe that story would disregard mine as false. What if they're right?

I struggled to my feet before the density and weight of my mood became too great to get out of my chair. Rising even a few feet above my sitting position was enough to see that my mood had fouled the atmosphere right around my chair. Standing above it, the world brightened. My story may or may not be right. But their story— *their story of unearned white male privilege and power*—cannot be right as it goes against life, against *biology and physics and harmony and against the meaning of life itself.*

That their story planted seeds of doubt in my story, made me choke. My story was simply going through a rough patch.

A quick check of my body found painful remnants of yesterday's long miles over uneven terrain in my knees and thighs, but also my feet. My fitful sleep had left me tired. Based on the sun's position, I guessed it was midafternoon and that I had a few more hours of daylight. My water mishap made me consider heading home a day early, a thought at odds with how weary I felt.

I put my pack back together, put it on, and walked west. Below me, the long reddish skirts flowing down from vertical cliffs, reoriented me. While moving along the canyon bottom was effortless, I wasn't going in the right direction, if such a thing existed. The route I sensed would take me where I needed to go, meant climbing down into the wash below me, then crossing at least one more.

The route into the next wash was without consequence except for a short friction section which tested my shoe rubber. The bottom showed signs of recent flow, so rather than climb directly out via an obvious route on the west side, I followed the canyon south, searching for water. Within minutes, I was walking in tiny capillaries trickling with water. The flow increased with the distance and I soon found where it had pooled deep enough to filter. I filled up three empty bottles. Moving again, I sensed my route was on the next layer above me. First, I needed to find a crack in the vertical side, an opening.

Eons of weather and floods had formed the wash into a curving rock tube, narrow enough to touch both sides at once. The further into it I walked, the deeper the wash became. After ten minutes, I came to a forty-foot pour-over. I back-tracked to a curve in the wash, where flood-fueled boulders had crashed, breaking the wall's smooth surface into cracks and sharp edges. I climbed them like rungs of a ladder. Reaching the rim, I faced a long nasty slog up steep red dirt.

As I would in deep snow, I picked a reasonable angle and started moving toward the summit I could see above me. My progress was too slow so, on all fours, I climbed straight up. I found a rhythm with my crawling. Exhausted, I could not stop, because if I rested, I would slide back down in the loose dirt.

I reached the top of the slope sweating like a pig. Part of the slope was stuck to my sweaty arms. I felt good, my heart pounding against the inside of my chest with perfect regularity. I reached for my throat and marveled as the pulse in my neck slowed. I'd passed the age that my mother died after her second open-heart surgery. Two years younger than I, my brother had undergone two heart surgeries in the past few years. After telling my doctor about my diet and walking and weightlifting, she said, "keep doing it; it must be working." Intuitively, I felt that the fatigue I felt after crawling to the top of that slope had nothing to do with blocked coronary arteries but simple effort. How quickly I recovered was the key for me. And feeling generally tired made sense based on what I'd done and how poorly I'd slept.

Looking out, I caught my breath—the trail, exactly where it was supposed to be.

A boulder the size of a small house was perched a hundred feet off the trail, and I decided to escape the heat in its shadow. I set up my chair and fell into it. I took out my book and water bottle (the good water, not the stuff I'd pulled out of that whitened canyon) and my third egg, leaving one for the next day's breakfast. Desperate, I reached into the bottom of my pack on the off chance I'd find a pen or even a pencil nubbin. Nothing but Coyote's shit bag. That and a petrified orange peel. I sank deep into my chair and looked out.

A raven flew over me and into a giant juniper fifty meters away. The joint cawing of a hundred pinion jays erupted the second the raven landed. The jays flew past me undulating in formation—a shape-shifting murmuration. The entire flock turned perpendicular to the sun, flashing their brilliant blue bodies.

I watched, aware of the winged movement in the distance in contrast to the stillness.

Then, in the corner of my eye, color: blue, not sky blue, and red, not subdued red-rock red but bright red. A young woman in blue shorts and a red long-sleeved top bounding up the trail with such energy, trying to keep up with the invisible force carrying her. Music I could not hear was surely playing in her ears and she was dancing to that music. I squinted and saw a mythical Indian runner carrying a message one hundred miles, overnight, difficult to track due to the great distance between her footprints. If I'd been visiting from outer space to explore and take information back to my far-away planet, my one 'sample' of life (besides birds and that lone moth) would be this young woman. I would assume Earth was a very happy place. She didn't look my way, and I stayed still, in case my altered reality had not made me invisible. I did not want to attract her attention. Seeing an old guy wearing a weird hat sitting in a chair in the shade of a large boulder in the middle of nowhere, would interrupt her bliss, something I did not want to do. I hoped that if she did see me that she wouldn't be afraid, but then women are constantly afraid when they're alone. I felt shame for my gender. The energy women waste worrying about their safety made me sick. How might that energy be better spent on creative approaches to the survival of our species? I wondered. The extinction of saber-toothed tigers largely freed men from this type of fear.

This thought signaled TIP ("Trump is President"), the First Demon. Twenty-seven women had accused our new president of sexual assault.

I could still hear the sound of her steps hitting the packed earth when the woman disappeared from my view. I thought about men I've known and whose work I respect, but who diminished and mistreated women, and/or were considered racist. The writers Ed Abbey and Jim Harrison came to mind, but there are many, most of them long gone.

The times in which these men thrived allowed behaviors which are now unacceptable. I feel differently about them than I do about the misogynist, racist Trump just elected president.

Must history ignore these men completely? Can I open the package on these men and pull out what is essential to me now and ignore the rest? What would these men be thinking now? How would they be acting? I judge men in power is based on their evolution. Trump is part of a large boy's club, men in power, stuck, refusing to change, lulled into floating through life on unearned privilege that has came free with their 'Y' Chromosome.

While I thought about men, the earth turned and moved my shadow. The sun began burning the back of my neck. I moved my chair.

Ed Abbey's possible evolution came to mind. A few years back, we were in Vermont at the White River Junction Film Festival to see "Wrenched," the film about Abbey and the Monkey Wrench Gang. Abbey talked about 'night work' the term he used to describe "sabotage" which he defined as "destroying property or dismantling machinery" to slow terrorism, which he defined as "acts of violence against life." It hit me: *the 'machine' is so much bigger, more expansive now, and difficult to define. And while the wilderness remains under constant threat, so is the entire planet. Had Abbey lived, I imagine that his idea of "Night work" would have evolved.*

For me 'night work" is that personal introspection required to know the full extent to which we're integrated with all life. Each of us has our unique piece of the machine to dismantle, and with 'night work' will discover what that piece is and how to deal with it.

By doing our night work, we'll know how the planet can make the best use of us.

The film ended. As Terry and I drove east toward the Connecticut River, I noticed a sign flashing a warning in the distance and remembered that the bridge was being repaired. When we got close enough to read the sign, I laughed out loud. "Night Work Begins", it said, referring to a future date. Yes, it flashed a warning, but not about the bridge. It was a warning from Ed, flashing in the darkness.

I took that sign (hell, it **was** a sign) that Ed was out there letting me know that he was out there, that he knew more dead than he had known while alive, that he would have changed.

More stillness, and then a pair of ravens tumbled horizontally right in front of me at high speed. They must be mating, I thought. Do they mate this time of year? Why do we automatically assume that other organisms enjoying one another are 'mating'? They disappeared to my left into the rocks at the base of the cliff. Perhaps they don't care what time of year it is. One of them, I'm assuming the male (I'm not sure why) swirled up into the sky in front of me as if something had been accomplished. He spiraled upward. He flapped his wings twice each cycle, and with each wing-flap he let out a deep chortle. The raven made seven circles before flying east. Had I not lost my pens, I'd have been writing in my book and missed that moment.

I dozed off until the shade moved again and the heat roused me. I thought about moving. My next challenge would be deciding where to camp that night. From where I sat, I saw a flat spot in the distance, up off to the west. I was moments from getting up when I heard the pitter-patter of feet and saw the young woman running down the way she'd come. I stayed quiet, still, and invisible as she passed.

I loaded my pack carefully, aware of the bag of Coyote shit in the bottom. I picked up my pack for the last time that day and dropped down to the trail. Where it turned right, I turned left, pulled by an invisible force into a small side canyon I'd have missed had I not been looking for a place to camp. I climbed over one low purplish slickrock dome and around another. Getting to the open flat spot I'd seen from my perch required close attention in just one spot—a tilted slickrock layer covered with small ball-bearing-like pebbles. Without one close call, I stepped onto the large open area where I would spend that night. It wasn't as flat as it seemed from the distance, but I found one spot just big enough for my camp between sage, blackbrush, and small juniper. I sat down where I planned on sleeping to check the views. In one direction, I looked down into a deep sensuous gorge as it turned purple in the lowering light. In the other, the vast cliff-lined wilderness. I'd spread out my stuff when I decided to spend the long dark hours until sleep around a small fire, something that hadn't crossed my mind the night before. Small sticks littered the area, which I hunted and gathered while wandering in circles. Near the edge of the area I defined as mine, I caught a rank odor when the breeze changed direction. Cat urine. Large cat urine. A mountain lion had just been seen in Castle Valley, on the street north of us. Walking Winslow the dog had become arduous, spending most of my time with him sniffing bushes to determine who had come into our territory and what that might mean for my safety (Winslow's primary concern). Earlier, when I told Laura, our friend and neighbor, that I was going for a long walk, she asked if I was taking my mask, referring to the poet Gary Snyder's suggestion that since big cats only attack from behind, wearing a mask on the back of one's head is a good precaution.

My trip took on a new dimension. My fire would supply both comfort *and* safety. I began living as if I was being watched.

I carried my second armload of wood to camp and added it to my growing pile. If I kept my fire small enough the twigs I'd gathered would last the evening. I adjusted the position of my camp so that I could sit and sleep between my fire and a car-sized boulder. I used the last daylight to look for other signs that I might be sharing the neighborhood with a mountain lion. Just beyond the western edge of my territory, I found the perfectly straight line of fresh cat tracks.

The cliffs above and beyond burned in the last sun. I settled into my chair with everything I needed within reach: to my right, my pile of twigs next to my stove and pan; to my left, the smooth hole I'd dug for my fire; in front of me my sleeping bag, positioned for me to pull it up around me when I got cold. On top of it, I'd placed my headlamp, book, hat, and gloves should they be needed.

I watched from my perch at the bottom of a darkening sea, the cliffs above lit by an interior fire. Each night the shadows rise like a purple tide, extinguishing the red cliff-glow, which the next morning's first light ignites from within.

After shuffling through my memory of similar evenings, I stopped at a specific moment two years before: A piece of sky freed itself from the grey grip of overcast clouds creating an opening through which a horizontal beam of sun shot, exploding when it hit the cliffs across the valley. I'd been in the dumps most of that day, unable to pinpoint any cause beyond the thick and relentless grey clouds, without a hint of sunlight. I soared when that bright flash squeezed into the narrow gap between cloud and clifftop, setting off a glowing yellow swath on the gentle slopes beneath the eastern walls. I sighed audibly, just recalling it, and sucked in a long breath. I realized how tied to these views, this light, I am. I'll never get used to the late-day sun hitting those cliffs, enlightening buttes above the darkening valley. How many photos have I taken of the different shades of orange and red, the different cloud backdrops? Evenings in Castle Valley provide a nearly constant and infinite source of awe. Awe ignites something physical inside of me as if it's a catalyst for a miraculous chemical reaction—a revelation.

I lit the stove to begin heating the alkaline water I'd found earlier in the day. The directions for preparing the "Cashew Curry" *Tasty Bite* says that the unopened foil envelope should be submerged in boiling water for five and a half minutes. I didn't have a watch, but since I would be heating but not actually cooking it, longer was preferable. I have a great little stove, one I always travel with for cooking soup if I get stranded in a blizzard. I've never read the list of ingredients on the *Tasty Bite* package, afraid of what I might find.

The air temperature plummeted, and I pulled on my parka. While the water heated, I built a six-inch-high twig castle in my fire pit. I'd found an old sales receipt in my pocket, wadded it up, and pushed it through the twig castle's front gate. I lit the edge of the paper, exploding it into a small ball of flame. By the time the water boiled on the stove, I had the most perfect fire ever built.

The sound of boiling water rattling the lid against the pan and the escaping wisps of steam were barely audible as the desert silence flowed in around me, growing denser with time.

The silence was thicker than my meal. I ate sacramentally. I fed the fire.

Darkness soon mixed with the silence, and the combination compressed the light from my fire into a small, glowing gem. I was warm in my comfortable seat, feeling pure contentment. I looked around for the Fourth Demon but couldn't find her.

I poured a bit of hot water from the pot into my cup and swirled it around to clean it. Then, to reward myself (for what I'm not sure), I made a cup of Italian Roast decaf using the remaining water. It smelled fine, but taking the first sip, my mouth reacted as though something had flown in from hell. I couldn't spit it out fast enough. No amount of treatment could have fixed that water. I tossed what remained in the cup over my shoulder beyond the fire, hoping it wouldn't land on anything living.

Checking my bottles, I realized that I had less than a quart of good water. I'd need a cup for morning coffee and half a cup for oatmeal and some to drink walking back home. I would brush my teeth without water.

My great fire burned bright and stung my left leg with its heat. Rather than move to escape my discomfort, I let the fire quiet for a few minutes. The nearly full moon cleared the cliff behind me, spreading its soft blue light into every space beyond the orange glow of the fire. My black shadow sat next to me. Two days later on the day before the actual full moon I would ask a number of people in Moab—at the grocery store, the liquor store, the transfer station—if they'd been out looking at the moon. Everyone had. ("I smoked a joint in the light of that moon." "We went for a night walk." "I stared at it directly above me 'till my neck got sore.") We join around the moon. Trump voters and Hillary voters, we all meet beneath the moon.

My woodpile had shrunk to one interesting stick. From where I sat, that last stick was a human arm bone complete with the elbow. The fire pulsed from red to orange to blue, and the heat from it rose in waves. Scientifically, there must be a formula able to predict the exact amount of time the fire would continue burning once I placed that last stick on the glowing coals: The size and density of the wood; air temperature; the speed of subtle breezes; the heat in the fire when I dropped in the last stick. Each of these factors could be given a value that could be multiplied, square-rooted, added to, subtracted from each other to calculate the 'time until absolute darkness.' Then I thought, "that would assume that time was constant," something I'd been thinking about lately.

I kept glancing down at my book with my headlamp light but wasn't in the mood to read. With no more wood to fuel it, the fire began a series of gasps, the gaps between them growing longer as the darkness deepened and thickened. Time cannot be constant. Someone—maybe Caesar, or hell, Noah—a long time ago must have surmised that a civil society depended on a constant rate of time. The moon appeared behind me; I could tell by the bright outskirts beyond the shadow my boulder formed in front of me. Was it 8 o'clock or nine? I wondered. And then why did it matter? I'd read about our biological rhythms—the natural timeframes in which we sleep, menstruate, etc. I believe that women usually make more sense, are less violent, more compassionate, etc., because every month their bodies remind them that biology plays the same powerful and miraculous role it has since the beginning of life. Men, I've read, have rhythms, too, albeit less obvious and rarely acknowledged.

Rhythms, cycles…the wild world has ten thousand, a million, as life pulses through time.

My leg, which had been burning earlier got cold, time to slip inside my sleeping bag. I made sure my water and headlamp were within reach and set my glasses on top of my book, where I'd know where to find them in the morning. When I thought I'd thought of everything, I pulled my bag up around me and laid down, still thinking about time.

Philosophers argue whether time is continuous, cyclical or linear, and if it goes in a constant direction. In my limited reading on the subject, I hadn't seen any argument as to its constancy. Yes, I know that according to our clocks, each hour is made up of sixty evenly spaced minutes, each day, 24 equal hours. The first time I wondered about how equal minutes were, I was exercising—doing timed intervals on my stationary bike. My timer says that the minute I go as hard as I can is equal to the minute that I rest, which seems ridiculous. The hard minute about kills me, while I wouldn't care if the resting minute went on forever. There are a thousand ways time is not constant. The most well-known is how the years move faster the older we get. And how slowly the years pass after a loved one dies and yet how quickly after the death of an acquaintance. ("I heard your mom died what was it? Three years ago?" "No, Brooke, it's been ten.") How time nearly stops while in a hospital waiting room. For me, time in the desert moves at the perfect pace, invisible were it not for the changing light. Not like work where either there's never enough time, or the days never seem to end. I never feel rushed in the desert, and never bored.

Long winter nights in the desert, however, take some getting used to.

My eyelids were getting heavy around the time I figured that the hours I would lay awake that night would seem three times as long as the hours I would sleep.

Regardless of what the philosophers say about time, I'm fairly sure it goes in one direction: Forward. Onward. No going back. Trump and his followers who what to "Make America Great, *Again*" want to go back. "Again" assumes that there was a time in the past when America was 'great' but is no longer. Since my first siting of a MAGA hat, I've wondered exactly when, in the past, "again" refers to. I sense that Trump and his many millions of followers, want to go back to post WWII. Women left the workforce to stay home where their husband ruled. They had well-defined roles: have babies. Take care of the family. Obey their husband. People of color knew their supporting role in American life, remaining segregated and dismissed. Indian people were a part of the past, not the present, a symbol for what had been conquered to give white people what they needed and deserved. White men were happy in control of their wives and children, their money, their government, their land.

Many Euro-Americans believe that they are supreme because they are white and therefore deserve political power, financial security, social mobility, *forever*, even if this means stopping time. But time does not stop. Today, white men are angry that time did not stop when they believed they were at the height of their power. The problems we see today seem to be rooted in the anger of white men who continue to believe they still deserve the stature they once had, that time took with it when it moved on. This anger became toxic once the frustration of losing most of what they bet on set in. They felt invisible. Trump came to power because he promised to turn back time. To help white men get back all they once had—*again*. But only if they fought for it. (Bring your guns.)

This paralyzed me. The fact that the TIP (Trump is President) demon came while I was fully conscious surprised me. That Demon YATT (You are Totally Toast) joined him scared me. Until then, YATT's role had been to inject me with worry by suggesting every danger I might face individually. For the first time, YATT came to warn about the havoc, death, and destruction Angry White Men might wreak on America.

We cannot go back in time, but what freaked me out was that the way forward is not set. I thought of aerial photographs showing how today the water in a river flows in a different channel than it did ten or a hundred years ago—moving toward the future by a constantly shifting route. A raven must have a better view of our future than we do.

I obsessed (again) about the unraveling of so much that I cared about—I was afraid that if I didn't get up, I might die in my sleeping bag. I wanted to sit up and look around, but the weight of a nameless demon was too much. As I'm prone to do with big insurmountable questions or problems, I divided the weight into smaller, more manageable pieces and focused on those closest to me: Besides Terry, the four things I care most about are:

+ Protecting wildness, landscapes, and species—against development and loss of habitat, but also the development of non-renewable resources.

+ Clean air and water and healthy food, all promised to us as inhabitants of this planet, and all threatened by corporate greed.

+ The safety and security of Louis and his family, which has become our family, and the safety and security of all those living on the margins, afraid every day; and

+ A future in which all life can thrive—now being threatened by the climate collapse caused by burning fossil fuels.

With the exception of global warming (which worsened with each part per million added to the greenhouse gases stored in the atmosphere), America was making slight improvements on these during the Obama Administration. Hillary Clinton promised more of the same. Trump, pandering to his angry base, promised the opposite: less pollution regulation, more corporate greed, less safety and security for non-Euro-Americans, and more burning of fossil fuels for power.

I could not wrap my arms around Trump becoming the face of what half of the American people think they want.

Hoping for the peace I needed to sleep, I created possible scenarios for moving past Trump.

First: He will hate the job, serve out his term, announce that he won't seek re-election, declare victory, and is rarely heard from again. *Highly unlikely.*

Second: His terrible life catches up with him, and he's impeached. This leaves Mike Pence for us to deal with. *Think "Fetus Funerals."*

Third: Trump, with the most radical, craziest Republicans on his side, announces re-election plans, although polls suggest he has little chance at another victory. Other Republicans grow a spine and throw their support behind one who might win. Mitt Romney comes to mind. *My demons get wiser, knowing all that's at stake.*

Fourth: Trump, god forbid, wins the 2020 election. And we wait four more years. The "erosion" of American democracy becomes "demolition". Gaia shudders and gasps.

Because of Bears Ears, I'd been thinking a lot about Indian People. Social media had been full of Native People protesting the Dakota Access Pipeline (DAPL) going across their sacred Lands, poisoning their water. For years, Terry and I had been engaged in the Bears Ears National Monument issue as allies of our Indigenous friends and neighbors. "A healing," it's been called. These issues have one thing in common: "It's time." It's time to "heal all our relations," according to Native People. Time to acknowledge the harm we white people have caused. Time for Euro-Americans to see and feel the power and importance of 'Sacred Lands,' something our white ancestors left behind when they came to America for "better lives." "It's time" for us to remember and discover and use all that we "know" in our bones, and not just what we're told. It's time to accept and embrace that life is moving— forward, onward, into an entirely new world, one dominated by the feminine. The hatred and violence accompanying the election was chiefly angry, desperate white men being forced to make room for the new world. At least, this is the idea that made me feel warm and good laying there waiting for sleep.

An entirely new, more feminine world. Imagine. Just then WHID (Second Demon, "What have I Done" with my life) showed up. "You've made your point," WHID said. "Now, do something about it."

I woke up depressed, the sun still hidden but its light turning black night into purple dawn. WHID had pestered me for hours about all the time I've spent in the darkness of Terry's shadow, how I'd become the lamenting victim who sacrificed too much, and worse, how it's too late to make up for lost time. Then the LISBB ("Life Is Beautiful, But...") demon showed up. She suggested that I'd made a choice, I'd entered her shadow willingly, and that now I had a new choice: I could beat myself up over it; or I could remember what I knew about the life force and evolution and adaptation and see my way beyond her shadow as my way of adapting to changing conditions. I would honor my time inside her shadow as training, as my apprenticeship, realizing, *remembering* what a gift she has been in my life, that there is no one on earth like her. But that we are all unique with different roles to play, each with our own path to follow. I thought back over the summer, listening to many readers tell her how she has inspired them and that her words have been life-changing. I felt proud of her for what she's accomplished and what we've done together. But not only do she and I have different roles in our evolving future, but different methods.

Stepping out of her shadow. I wondered if this was what I needed to do to move on personally or if this is what the planet now requires of me. Or if there's a difference.

After boiling a cup and a half of my dwindling water supply, I ate the delicious improv (boiled egg/maple oatmeal) breakfast, then cleaned up with a small, perfect cup of coffee.

All I'd needed to survive was spread out over a space the size of a twin bed. I marveled at how little I actually needed, then sighed, thinking back to what I found in that rank storage room I'd cleaned out earlier. *So much stuff. How? Why? All we can't let go of.*

I packed all my gear, placing Coyote's bag on top, thinking I'd dump it before I got home. I was up and moving in ten minutes.

"Marvelous," I thought, moving up the trail from my camp. Marvelous how after only a few days of hard work, my body felt young and vigorous, as if I could walk forever.

I moved toward the pass on an invisible current. I was excited about being home with Terry, entering an unknown future together in a brand-new context. After forty-one years together. Poised.

An insect buzzed by in the just-heated air reminding me of the first night's moth and the peppered evolutionary moths. Evolution is adapting to changing conditions. If the election of Donald Trump's is not a 'changing condition', I can't imagine what is. "How do we evolve in order to adapt?" is the big question. All the peppered moths had genes for both light and dark colors. The gene for light color was "dominant," making the white moths invisible to their bird predators who ate the dark moths easily found sleeping on the white lichen-covered trees. When carbon pollution covered trees with soot, the white moths became easy prey. The dark moths survived, and this gene, once hidden and recessive, became dominant.

That this story kept coming back to me in deeper and deeper detail meant that it had power I needed out there in the desert. We all have visible and invisible traits and strengths. Trump has darkened the world and the future, and now our invisible traits have become the tools for our survival. This story fits with my theory—that the collective which we tap by being out in the wilds has the evolutionary tools we've always needed and used to save ourselves. What is 'recessive' in me—hidden—that must, if we're to survive, rise toward the light and become dominant?

The biggest evolution/adaptation may be that those of us who love wildness, who crave natural beauty, can no longer be outside without asking, "How can we be of the most use?" The answer will come, in the wind, in the current of the river, in the sound the raven's wing makes cutting through the solitude. It was there with me. I could hear it. "This will be my job from now on." I thought. "Encouraging this."

I flowed down from the pass, past the cave, and back on Coyote's path, onward toward home. Before passing through the portal, I stopped knowing that I would be moving from one world to the other, between realities. The portal seemed blocked by an invisible-yet-impenetrable force field. Would I recognize the world on the other side? Everything had changed. No longer will my skin color, my gender, my nationality protect me. As if the threats to life on this planet are a pathogen that has just mutated, the immunizations and vaccinations we've spent years developing are now useless.

If time spent in wild solitude is the path into the vast collective unconscious, then I need to remember what I've heard wafting on the breeze. I must waste no more time.

The pressure inside the portal eased and I pushed through it, knowing that my future lay spread out on the other side, my home and my dog, and Terry where we'll work side by side, both of us in the full force of light.

I felt the portal close behind me but did not look back.

My post-election walkabout ended in the way that all my walks in the wilderness end. I arrived home ebullient, excited about life, confident, renewed. Surely, I thought, Trump's role is to expose America's fetid, toxic underbelly, which we all assumed had disappeared forever. I felt light and strong and moved smoothly throughout the house. I emptied my pack in the garage and, as I began putting my gear away, noticed Coyote's shit bag. Passing through the portal had converted its contents into an elastic knee brace and an Ace bandage.

Terry caught me up. People had already taken to the streets. "Not my President," their signs said, referring to all we knew about his despicable life, but none of what we would soon learn.

I checked the pump room. Cleaning it out had not deterred the rat. I found more insulation, colorful notecards which had been chewed along their edges, and a small screwdriver.

Terry had finished a long poem she'd begun on the bank of the Colorado River, the morning after the election, the words flowing like water. She's shown me that writing honestly about anything creates clarity because you cannot look away once you face what stands before you. Fear bows to courage.[4] This may be why our early ancestors felt safer eye-to-eye with *Dinofelis*, that saber-toothed cat who made humans their main meals, than they did wondering about each shadowed sound they heard coming from behind..

WALK TWO

NOVEMBER 4 - NOVEMBER 7, 2020

FOR MONTHS I'D HOPED that the Presidential Election, Tuesday, November 3, 2020, would be the end of Trump and the beginning of anything else. But I wasn't sure. And, unlike the 2016 Election, the 2020 election was too close to call. Falling asleep on Election Night, my body tensed in preparation for another four years of Trump. But, somehow, my mind was calm compared to four years before.

The polls people predicted that while Trump may lead early, he would eventually lose once all the mailed-in votes were counted. Deep down beneath it all, I would discover that the calm I felt had nothing to do with Trump and everything to do with our own extinction as a species—the trajectory we've been on since the beginning of civilization. I felt the calmness of having accepted the inevitable.

While listening to media updates about vote counting in close states, I gathered the gear I would need to spend a few days out in the desert as I did in 2016.

I packed my rucksack with food and stove, water, sleeping paraphernalia, and the satellite emergency tracker I bought as a compromise after Terry insisted that I was too old to be going off backpacking alone. If I'm incapacitated for any reason, I push a button on this little phone-sized machine, and rescuers show up to save me. I felt safer knowing I would have it. I did think of that great conservationist, Randy Udall, who in 2013 while backpacking alone in the Wind Rivers, dropped dead mid-stride from a heart attack or stroke and wasn't found for a week. An emergency transponder wouldn't have helped.

I'd planned to leave on Friday, hoping that by then the Election would have been 'called.' Checking the weather, however, I decided Thursday morning that I would leave later that day, returning Saturday, ahead of the forecasted storm.

Before leaving, I checked the rat room and discovered more packrat activity, which always picks up as temperatures drop. This time she'd brought in three pens and the cigarette lighter I'd looked for in vain, forcing me to buy a new one for my hike. I realized just how smart this little scamp is. Earlier, I'd piled soft-ball-sized stones around what appeared to be her entrance. I noticed that although the rocks seemed too heavy for even the largest rat to move, she'd managed. She'd dug out at the base of each stone, destabilizing it. After moving out of the way, she watched as the stone, fueled by gravity, dropped into the hole she'd dug, creating a previously impossible opening.

The pundits kept talking, somehow able to pull from thin air details of those last few votes, which would make the difference. Finally, I asked Terry to drop me at the place where ordinary reality becomes non-ordinary. This would save me the 45 minutes of the daylight walking across the flats would take.

My plan was to pass through the Portal, walk up Coyote's trail, and over the pass into the wilderness, beginning my 2016 hike in reverse. I loved where I'd spent my last night four years earlier and was confident that I could find it again before dark.

"Right here," I said, after we'd driven ten minutes. She stopped and we got out. I shouldered my pack, kissed her, and walked off up the wash, which still basked in orange light. Terry drove off as the west rim shadow passed over us.

Moving quickly, I do a quick inventory: Bad, bad knee: feeling OK…7.5 out of 10. Bad Good knee: 10. Lungs: fine. Pack: just right. My feet feel good.

Mentally, I feel strong and vital. Even the specter of another four years of Trump has had little effect. This surprises me, considering the extra weight of his 2016 win I drug behind me on my earlier trip.

I have goals for my walk: I will concentrate on being open, hoping that what I know to be true will occur: the wild lifeforce—that treasure trove of survival contained in the collective unconscious which I'd come to trust, gives me what I need, regardless of what I want. I will try not to think much. I will move and sit and watch. And breathe and dream.

Besides weekly re-supply trips into town and two trips to Salt Lake City for family, we'd stayed within a few miles of home since March—eight months.

My Pandemic universe, which I'd mapped, is contained within a rough circle. The Portal sits in the center. Round Mountain marks the far southern Edge. Porcupine Rim forms the western boundary. To the north, spectacular Moenkopi slopes angle up toward Wingate cliffs and formations. I explored the canyons and climbed the soft ridges on a few cloudy days this past oh, so hot summer, much of it choked by smoke from 5 million acres burning across the American West. I'd attempted to reach "the Petrified Flame"—a small, almost toothlike vertical sandstone outcropping that stands prominently on the valley's north rim. This 'Flame' is one of those formations I always marvel at: how on earth has something this delicate survived the same forces (wind, rain, freezing, thawing, and time) that formed this massive valley?

The main entrance into Castle Valley rises up from the Colorado River through the red eroding hills, passing through a seam (which I sense was man-made) before dropping into the Valley. The Loop road runs south, separating the town from the eastern slopes and cliffs. The valley has two other entries: one from the southeast and Gateway Colorado; the other to the west from Spanish Valley, south of Moab. The road up and over the LaSal Mountains was the original wagon route to Moab. The Colorado River forced its way to the edges of its canyon, leaving no room for a road between water and cliff. The first way in was a trail in the northwest corner, up to the rim and across the plateaus, in and out of the canyons. I walked it once. It took all day. Now, thanks to dynamite and modern machinery, Highway 128 runs smoothly along the remodeled cliffs.

Although the border separating ordinary and non-ordinary reality shifts and moves and cannot be mapped, the Loop Road is good physical approximation. While the coronavirus shrunk my world if measured by physical space, it also weirdly expanded it in terms of depth and meaning. Beyond length and width, Castle Valley has grown in dimension—meaning, magic, and possibility.

During the early days of isolation, I was frustrated, wondering when this disruption might end. Now I feel both gratitude and guilt, living in such a place—knowing that hundreds of thousands of fellow citizens are suffering and dying from COVID-19 due to the government's choice to protect the economy and not the health of those over which it governs.

Recently, a friend told me the story of an old hermit living beyond the edge of a village. Once during a famine, a pilgrim came to him saying, "We are hungry. What should we do?" The hermit said, "Well then, let us fast." I love this. It helped me accept that isolation was necessary to control the virus. I could choose how I would deal with the isolation: like it or hate it. We've been warned. "You need to stay home, isolate yourself." This is a different kind of famine, and yes, we are hungry in a different way. "Well, then, let us be hermits."

We don't work in the grocery store, the post office, the bookstore, and Amazon warehouse as our son, Louis, does, or in other 'essential businesses". We are not frontline healthcare workers, risking our lives daily. The best we can do is stay home.

We have chosen to live as close to wildness as possible.

Being close to wildness is often associated with being 'far' from the work required to 'make a living' in modern society. We've had to adjust our lives accordingly—move around a lot, commute, taking work away from home periodically, teaching here, speaking there. We've lucky that although the pandemic has washed away a large chunk of our work, what remains can be done online. The unexpected gift and privilege has been being home to chart the seasonal changes.

Our gratitude is immense—to those risking their health and their lives to provide for all of us confined to our homes. The UPS driver who drops off both necessities and luxuries on our doorstep. Those who keep the shelves stocked, who ring up our purchases at City Market and the Moonflower CO-OP, those amazing Castle Valley women who weekly pick up and deliver food to those too vulnerable to shop on their own; those who process and deliver our mail, who pack and send our packages at the mailing center, who deal with our trash and recycling at the transfer station; and those bookstore employees who make sure those needs are met. All those who provide our communication, our heat and light, and water. For the farmworkers who grow our food. We are grateful for the heroes in the hospitals who take care of those of us who have and will have COVID-19, and who will help some of us die. This is not a passive act. We are praying again, which for us means making the simple gesture of lighting candles at night to honor and remember, and bowing daily in front of Round Mountain. We're both over sixty years old and more susceptible to the virus. While we've been moved when asked by younger people if we need our food delivered, we've declined. The least we can do is become hermits. In Hindu philosophy, all humans ideally mature into hermits.

For years, I've wondered about the role 'hermits' have played throughout human history. If there is a 'hermit wisdom'—and I believe there is—it can be accessed by walking. Besides solitude and scarcity and choosing to live close to nature rather than in a city, walking is a key factor in the eremitic life.

There's walking, but then there's wandering. Walking is a means of getting from one place to the next. In contrast, wandering is an end in itself. Wandering is goalless, open-minded. In my own experience, wandering is directly related to imagination and creativity—and, I believe, my spiritual evolution. When my ideas run out or no longer serve me, I go wandering in the desert to gather more.

On my "Pandemic Universe" map, I've labeled this route, Coyote Path—it's roughly the trail Coyote guided me along to my Shamanic cave. It's one of the seven routes included on my map.

+ Hermit Mile (various, near the house)

+ The Green Gate walk.

+ Coyote Path.

+ Coyote Path Redux.

+ Grunt and Burp (actually, "Grunt, Burp, and Fart).

+ Horse Trail.

+ Walking the Wire (the route that follows the old barbed wire fence).

My universe is divided into four worlds: Hermit world; Enchanted World (where anything not *illuminated* has been *eliminated*); Middle World ("the Flats" between Hermit and Enchanted world); and Distantworld ("There be Dragonflies). Many features I've encountered throughout the years have taken on higher—symbolic, archetypal—value, such as Cave NOLAC ("Cave that is 'no longer a cave'), Portal (access from Midworld to Enchanted World), Pink Gate, and Invisible Gate (access between Hermit World and Midworld; Green Gate (entrance to the vast home of Queen, the Erotic Juniper); Skull Bush; And the Enchanted Forest.

While the work of Carl Jung has always fascinated me, it has become a major influence and anchor during COVID isolation. He believed in two worlds, "the *inner* world…truly infinite" and "in no way poorer than the *outer* world." During my walks, most occurring in the outer world, the line between it and the inner world, blurs. My walking has taken on mythical dimensions. My walking has been wandering.

I brush against sage heavy with seed as I drop into the wash. Once loose, the sage pollen forms a visible cloud. "Such a rush of gladness," I say out loud as I breathe in the yellow air. I doubt I've ever used the word "gladness" before.

Feeling loose and light, I almost jog up the gulch. Stopping briefly at the Cave Which is no Longer a Cave, I notice that the meltwater from the recent snow has formed sensuous curves in the sand while passing the mouth. Three years ago, I discovered that what I'd earlier thought was the solid back of my Shamanic Cave had been generations of dirt, which had washed away during a recent strong storm. What had been my Shamanic

Cave had become a tunnel filled with light. My Shamanic cave was no longer a cave. I recalled our trip to Turkey. We visited Cappadocia where a strange geologic phenomenon compressed volcanic ash into 'fairy chimneys' which reminded me of the hoodoos at Bryce Canyon and Goblin Valley, and created massive buttes and mesas, which have been hollowed out for homes and churches. We visited one cliff with an extensive city within it, where for decades, hundreds of Christians hid out from the Romans, making wine and breathing air through the same sophisticated ventilation system used today by the thousands of tourists visiting this spectacular place. The cave churches have arches and niches and walls covered and recovered by haunting religious art. Terry and I spent a week with guides exploring the area. We'd been oohing and awing the art painted onto the walls of one fantastical church when I wandered into a room which had been roped off—not part of the tour. It was dark and damp, and as I stood there waiting for my eyes to adjust, a familiar feeling came over me: I'd been there before. The room was empty and completely blackened as if a fire had burned through it. I stepped over the rope and walked into the middle of the room, and turned in a circle looking for the source of my feeling. Halfway around, it hit me: Coyote's cave. Chills shot up my neck. My Shamanic cave. I'd been to that room many times during my shamanic journeys. My cave had been cleansed by fire.

I race on, the cliff shadow moving fast behind me. At the pass, I drop my pack and grab my pile jacket from the top. I know the cold that shadow carries and I'll be ready.[5] While I'm at it, I'll check my cyanometer. Since the sky is so blue, I'll measure it. Terry found me a print of the famous cyanometer Horace Bénédict de Saussure made in 1760 to document the color of the sky—Alexander von Humboldt, the heroic German explorer, carried one throughout his travels. I couldn't figure out how to use it without cutting it up, so I made my own using various blue paint chips from the local hardware store. Today the sky is approximately "Mystic Blue" (6G4). Perfect. But then my cyanometer has only 12 shades of blue, nowhere near enough. de Saussure's has 49.

If color can be felt, I feel the purple as the shadow's edge passes between my legs and then over me while I look out over the vast wilderness. The shadow is a rogue wave in a massive dark ocean, which becomes a blanket, thickening the air as it covers my route. The distant Fisher Towers stand tall in the last of the sun. I shoulder my pack and head down the trail, which has dried from the recent snow. Memory is strange and has layers, and I search mine for remnants of my first post-election hike, clues as to where to leave the trail to find my spot. I'd found my camp by accident in 2016, and looking for it now, four years later, I wonder if I can find it.

Worried that I have missed the small canyon which leads to my camp, a huge familiar boulder appears in front of me. I immediately recalled the hot afternoon I spent reading in its shade. I'm but a few minutes from my destination.

Now everything is familiar. I hurry up the small wash carved into the smooth purple sandstone and climb a sloping wall, all of which I recognize. I wonder how I camped here on such tilted ground. Ten meters away, there it is: a narrow flat spot made of rich red sand, the desert dropping away steeply to the west into a narrow spectacular gorge. Four years of wind, rain, snow, and blistering sun has obliterated any sign of me.

I set my pack down against exactly the same boulder I'd set it against before. There it is, unburned four years ago, that last stick like a human bone, an arm, complete with elbow. It is surrounded by small chunks of burned wood from my long-time ago fire.

How little has really changed. How quickly this place has been restored. In the long story, in deep time, perhaps the damage of these past four years will disappear just as the remnants of my last time camped there had.

My plan to camp where I'd spent my last night in 2016 is my only plan. I realize at least one way I've changed in four years. Back then, I'd mapped out an impressively—and it turns out, impossibly—a large and long route, involving cliffs and canyons and river crossings. I'd accomplished only part of it. As the map of my universe has changed, so have my desires and expectations. No longer concerned with physical distance, my plan this time is for more depth and clarity, which time in the wilderness provides. This is the dimension of wildness I spend much of my time trying to understand. The wilderness I've planned to explore on this walk-about is only the means. Wildness is the end.

"There really were people who preferred wilderness to civilization. This is the basis for the hermit tradition wherever it is found." I'd memorized this quote from *The Road to Heaven:*

Encounters with Chinese Hermits, by Bill Porter, a.k.a. "Red Pine." While trying to understand 'hermits' I realized that the wisdom for which they were sought out was embedded in the wild landscapes they inhabited. This was the beginning of my quest to understand, qualify, and quantify the value of wild places to modern humans.

Civilization has become off-limits during the pandemic. I've chosen to spend my time in the wilderness, which suggests that, according to one definition, I've become a hermit. Before the pandemic, wilderness was my antidote to civilization. During the pandemic wilderness has all but replaced civilization. I now call this pandemic "The Hermit Virus."

The vast view surrounding my camp has not changed since my last visit. I love wilderness and have spent most of my life looking for ways to protect more of it. Lately, I'm becoming ambivalent. In most cases, lack of federal protection means development (in Utah, this translates to carbon— oil, gas, coal) which destroys the wild character of a place. But now, designation brings with it publicity and hordes of us seeking adventure who contribute a different kind of damage. Land protection, these days, means choosing between the lesser of evils. The Mary Jane Wilderness spreads out before me in all directions. I'm not sure when or if I've crossed the exact line, separating regular life from a landscape officially meeting all the criteria to be officially designated, "Wild". Usually that line only exists on maps. Personally, that "line" shifts back and forth, and in and out of existence. A bit like the line between "ordinary" and "non-ordinary" reality. Perhaps they're the same line.

The Mary Jane "Unit" is included in the "Citizen's Proposal", having been eliminated from the Bureau of Land Management Inventory because it lacked "opportunities for solitude". Recalling this now makes me chuckle.

All these places need re-naming. I have nothing against Mary-Jane Richardson, who with her husband, Dr. Sylvester Richardson (after whom "Professor Valley is named") home-steaded this valley in the late Nineteenth Century. Strange, I think, naming a wild place after the white people who settled it.

In contrast, "Bears Ears", is named for twin buttes on the head of a giant bear gazing out over the landscape. They are found in stories told for generations by Hopi, Diné, Ute, and Zuni people, each with a word in their language which trans-lates to "Bears Ears".

Melting snow from the recent storm has soaked the sand during the warm days. At night the cold draws that moisture into its darkness, leaving the surface soft and airy. I unload my pack and spread my sleeping bag and pad out on the same spot as before. I roll out my camp chair two feet from the boulder that, although tilted, will be my table. I set up the stove and pot and food between the chair and the boulder and carve out a small crater where I will build a fire. Then I wander out beyond my perimeter to find dead wood to burn. My timing, though unplanned, is perfect, and I am able to set up in the last light of day.

If Bears Ears are atop the head of a giant bear a hundred miles from here, this is the Bears chest and I am here inside the heart of the same Bear. The Bears Heart pumps lifeforce to the full expanse of its body through this network of tiny canyons. On my map, I will write, "Bears Heart". My name for this place is "Heart of the Bear Wilderness." "Why not?" I ask myself.

President Obama, in one of his last major decisions, designated "Bears Ears National Monument" on December 28, 2016, just weeks before Trump's inauguration. Due to the widening gap between the two sides of the wilderness issue, Presidents have historically used the Antiquities Act to protect significant places once all public processes have failed. Such was the case with Bears Ears.

Obama's stunning proclamation prioritized the area's cultural brilliance, as we all hoped and believed it would.

For hundreds of generations, native peoples lived in the surrounding deep sandstone canyons, desert mesas, and meadow mountaintops, which constitute one of the densest and most significant cultural landscapes in the United States. Abundant rock art, ancient cliff dwellings, ceremonial sites, and countless other artifacts provide an extraordinary archaeological and cultural record that is important to us all, but most notably the land is profoundly sacred to many Native American tribes, including the Ute Mountain Ute Tribe, Navajo Nation, Ute Indian Tribe of the Uintah Ouray, Hopi Nation, and Zuni Tribe.

The entire process cast light on a very fragile and important place, attracting many who may or may not have appreciated the depth of meaning attached to this place. Those of us who trust the process bet that any damage done by those coming to visit Bears Ears before any planning or funding would be far less than that from the fracking planned for the area.

For me, protecting Bears Ears took on a greater significance than previous wilderness Issues. Normally, we argue our pro-wilderness position based on ecological preservation, biological, geographic, and geological uniqueness, and the economic potential of the human-powered recreation. Bears Ears is different. Bears Ears is acknowledging, honoring, and then protecting land that is sacred to Native people who have lived there for many generations and who live there now. I hear Jonah Yellowman's voice again: "It is time." Recently, he said to Terry and me, "we are not just protecting Bears Ears for our people, but for all people." Bears Ears inspires me to consider the sacred in my own life.

The distant setting sun lights up one side of Sister Superior, a spectacular sandstone formation above me, hijacking all of my attention. Glow or reflect? "Glowing" is being lit from within. "Reflecting" is interception and then radiating back external light toward its source without absorbing it. This may apply not only to towering stone formations but people. "Glowing" seems unintentional, is unconscious, just happens. "Reflecting" requires consciousness and the desire to give back the illumination received, akin to 'grace.'

The contrast of the one side set on fire by the setting sun, with the other in darkening shade, stuns me. The two sides are connected to one another like the two covers of an open book. "Stunned," I've discovered, is to be momentarily interrupted, in this case by beauty. By awe. *Pay attention to what attracts my attention, to what 'flirts' with me. In nature, this is the source of 'awe.'*

Awe must be a factor in what is sacred—stunned by the setting sun lighting a tall rock on fire. Yes. This moment.

Finding perfect wood is difficult. It consists mainly of small chunks of dead juniper partially covered by red sand. I recall wood being difficult to come by before and feel lucky to find what I do. Carrying an armload back to camp, I look down into the gorge where a small dead tree is lodged in a crack on a ledge. I appreciate the uncommon symmetry of its long intact branches reaching upward even in death. I stack my wood close enough to reach from my chair but not close enough to the fire to accidentally ignite. I retrace my steps to that tree and gather twigs and sticks it has shed, laying around it.

The tree is a pinion pine. Its perfect wood is hard yet brittle enough to break by hand.

Needing tiny twigs, I break off the dead ends from the tips of a Cliff Rose branch. I wonder if I am helping the bush in the way that pruning a rose bush helps it.

We, modern humans, are at the far most outer edge of the Tree of Life. (You know the one...the earliest life forming the trunk, then different major branches the different major classes of life, dividing and dividing through time, plants separate from animals, invertebrates and vertebrates—different forks.) Out on the far edge of the canopy, there we are, modern humans, the smallest, outermost twigs, the tip of life. Earlier in the summer, I asked Kara, the plant lady in our community, why the sumacs I'd transplanted weren't doing well. "Prune them," she said. "Cut them way back." I cut away all the twigs, leaving only the large, central stock. This worked, and soon, tiny green buds appeared, later becoming leaves on the ends of new branches.

"*Pruning.*" From the Oxford English Dictionary: *To cut or lop off what is superfluous to promote fruitfulness.* The Tree of Life. Something goes extinct, a twig out on the canopy's far edge, pruned, by who knows what force—loss of habitat, exotic new predator, climate change. Does the branch from which the twig sprung become more 'fruitful? Will the new growth be different? No doubt pruning the modern human twig will help the rest of the tree.

Waves of liquid darkness spread across my world as I separate my wood into three piles: small (twigs), medium (branches, breakable into six-inch-long pieces); and large (too big to break).

I put on all my warm clothes, fire up my headlamp, and sink into my chair. Everything I need is here.

In the crater I've dug to my left, I build a perfect mound of twigs. It looks like a human skull that bursts into flame within seconds when I flick my lighter into its mouth I've left at the base. I add more twigs and then small branches. Turning to my right, I light my tiny stove and place the pot I've half-filled with water. The fire burning, the pot not quite boiling, I sit and stare into the darkness. Nothing can hurt me. I've not thought of the election since finding my camp.

Four years ago, I was so distraught by the election that I felt that all I had left was to go walk in the wilderness and made the decision in the spur of a moment. Then, I needed to sort out my feelings, make some plans, find some invisible context. More than anything, I needed distraction. I needed intense physical activity and wild beauty, and even discomfort to take me into the essence of things—away from all the noise, the terrible truth, and the nightmare we faced.

Although the stakes are higher now than four years ago, I feel differently. I wonder what kind of country will exist once the votes are counted. Once I get home. This time, I know we will weather whatever comes next. America is engaged in change.

I've always *known* unconsciously that something good, something wise is transmitted to us up from the earth while we wander in wild places. During the past four years, I've attempted to name that knowledge, so I can use it.

Years ago, while responding to *The Story of My Heart* by Richard Jefferies, the 19th Century British nature/mystic, I was struck to learn that while well-read, his family was poor, and he was not well-educated. His revolutionary and timeless wisdom must have come up from the earth through the bottoms of his feet. "The air," he wrote, "the sunlight, the night, all that surrounds me seems crowded with inexpressible powers, with the influence of souls, or existences, so that I walk in the midst of immortal things."

The Earth does give off a force.[6] The "Schumann Resonance" pulses at 7.83 Hertz per second. The earth's lifeforce is a pulse that pushes information up from the middle of the Earth. The Yuan-chauny is a place near the ball of our foot through which we absorb that force—that knowledge—with each step we take.

The stove hums as fire's heat reaches my legs. I add more twigs and marvel at the height of the flames, twice the diameter of the twig-skull I'd made.

Being slightly confident about the final outcome of the election contributes to my calm, but there is more to it. I've been through many emotions during the months—hell, the years—leading up to November 3rd, everything from we're doomed to authoritarian rule to how excited I'll be with a Democratic landslide. I left the house knowing that while Biden/Harris had gained a slight lead, I carry the weight of reality that over 72 million people voted for Trump. I know many of them—some are family. They are not stupid or easily brainwashed. I feel calm and not depressed or angry, knowing there was little I could have done to change anyone's mind, in the same way, I know they could not have hoped to change mine.

Days before the election, I wrote to Bill Porter (Red Pine): *….Trying to be clear-headed about the election but finding that difficult. Any advice? In my saner moments, I see the day after the results are known the same as the day before. At other times, not sure. Baking a chocolate cake.*

His response:
Apparently, tomorrow is our last day of this hiatus (at this point, I thought he was talking about America, politics, the election…but) *in the unusual onslaught of*

rain and cold. One more hike is planned before it all ends. I'm sure this election means a lot to a lot of people. But I'm not so sure, whatever the outcome, their happiness or sadness will be but momentary.I personally expect some euphoria. Then a long, cold, dismal winter. That could be a good thing. But people never stop thinking they can legislate happiness. I'm looking forward to spring already...
Bill.

I live in a cocoon. Who will be our next president may not be known for days, but even if Biden prevails, this country is no longer mine. That the election was even close suggests that I have little or nothing in common with half of America. And that half, much of it high-school educated, non-reading, white, gun-owning—is so distant from me that I forgot it existed beyond small festering corners. That I feel less badly than in 2016 says something about the state of decay we've experienced these past four years. But also that regardless of who the next president is, the great division will remain. Who the next president will be pales in importance to the basic question of life. *Do we believe we're one species among many and subject to the laws of nature and physics, and thermodynamics? Or that we're superior to other life and exempt from natural processes?*

I'm glad I'm not younger and might miss the worst horror scenarios being predicted. I bleed for the generations coming behind ours and the endurance and energy they may need for basic survival. We know what we're up against now. Trump was so new to us four years ago. Now his specter will be my test:

how much of my energy do I want to spend on anger, frustration, and hate?

I feel as I did many years ago realizing I could no longer be a Mormon. Relief? Yes, but also loss. The loss of belonging. The loss of belonging to the religion that has formed our family foundation for five generations. The loss of belonging to a country that once prided itself in being the greatest on earth, with an inspired constitution. With freedoms not found anywhere else. Then, I left the Mormon Church. Now, America has left me. My hero Wendell Berry once wrote, "You can love your country and hate your government." I love the American Earth, not America, right now.

Red Pine helped, saying that true happiness cannot depend on who wins or loses an election. I'm still ambivalent—if I achieve an inner happiness independent of anything happening around me, what will motivate me? Would I be be involved in making necessary changes? Will I do my part to offset the environmental damage resulting from my privilege? How would I feel if I wasn't secure and stable? If I had to scrape and scramble to simply feed my family? Inner peace, regardless of one's outer circumstance, is the goal. My *inner happiness* is an option because so many of life's other details have been worked out for me over many generations of white privilege.

I'd gone to bed election night hoping not to let the results *over which I'd had little control* 'legislate' my happiness. I still feel that way, sitting between fire and stove, steam escaping from my pot. I vibrate between believing that I know what I'm doing and rationalizing that I spend my life doing nothing of value. Oh well. Right now, at this moment, I am present, my demons nowhere near.

Red Pine's response to my anxiety going into the election was based on his ability to see what is occurring around him within the context of deep time. I'm beginning to understand this. His response caused me to back out for a broader view. I have much to learn if I am ever to see Red Pine's view. In my broadening view, Trump is so small that he has disappeared. Still in view is the force that produced him that has no further use for democracy. But lurking, blurred in the grey beyond the light, is something else.

The spore. Recall the ant, having inhaled the spore of a small mushroom, begins acting strangely, until it does what it's not done before, climbing to the tip of the highest grass blade, where it dies, the new mushroom generation, bursting from its head.

Half of the country seems to have inhaled the spoor. They are on their way up the grass. Then two terrible questions to contemplate: *When will their heads finally explode?* And *What about the next generation?*

There has been the bottle of simmering frustration, which once Trump uncorked it, has flowed out as hatred. Although Biden was not my first choice for President, he may be the person these times call for. He can't replace the cork. And re-bottling all the recently unleashed hatred is impossible. The best hope might be that he's able to build from this rubble of a country, a new platform on which those who choose to, regardless of history or party or philosophy, might stand together. I might be dreaming.

Already, before the final results are known, there are those calling for us to reach out to the other side. I am not ready.

I see no meeting of minds with people on the other side of this divide, those convinced that our democracy threatens their supremacy. Middle ground is too far away to see. I'm not sure how I'll act if forced to face people I care about but can no longer trust—these men or the women[7] they control. One thing I thank the pandemic for is the excuse it's given me to stay put.

With Obama, the first Black man elected President, the pendulum swung further to the left than ever before. As pendulums do, it swung back just as far to the right with Trump. If he wins, Joe Biden might (just might) be able to slow the pendulum, contain some of its momentum as it swings back, shortening its arch. But a pendulum cannot be stopped.

If Trump and his people are out there on the right at farthest point on the pendulum, that "extreme position" is masculine. The worst of masculinity. White, toxic masculinity. The swing back then will inevitably involve the feminine. We see this with Senator Kamala Harris, Biden's pick for Vice President. *It is time* for this, too, I think. Way past time.

At a conference in California a few years ago, I heard those words again, "It is time," this time by Illarrio Merculieff, an Inuit leader from Alaska.

"Hell," I recall thinking, "it *really* must be time," as chills covered my body. Merculieff talked about having traveled the world meeting with Indigenous leaders. "We realized," he said, "that we all thought we had the complete story when we really only had a piece of the story." "Now", he went on, "we have the complete story, and *it is time* to share it with the world."

The complete story. Illarrio proceeded to tell the story of the return of the 'Sacred Feminine' without which our survival into the future is questionable.

Humans worshipped the sacred feminine for most of our history, until recently with the advent of agriculture. Agriculture, manifest destiny, modernity all required suppressing the feminine, which had brought wisdom, peace, and higher consciousness to all people.

Illarrio believes that as men, our highest and best use will be to clear the way for women to do their real work, to protect what is sacred. Personally, I look to Jung here, who would say that men, too have a feminine side called the *anima*. Part of our role as men is to focus on that dimension of ourselves.

I drop the foil envelopes containing the curry and the chipotle rice into the pot of boiling water. All of my thinking and preparing my food has taken up too much of my mental capacity, and I've neglected my fire, which has gone out. I place four six-inch pieces of the pinion onto the coals and wait and hope that the night breeze enflames just one of the glowing coals.

With an tiny audible explosion, fire erupts from the middle ember, and the smoke rises from the stick pile, billowing to the east in large blue-grey pillows, which disappear into the darkness.

I finish dinner, reheat the water, and make a cup of de-café. Since I did not make the mistake of dropping my pens this time, I jot down random thoughts in my notebook bathed in the light of my headlamp.

When I reach out to drop yet another stick on my fire, the black parka covering my arm attracts my attention. Actually, I don't have everything I need. I don't have my amazing Hermit parka. I left it back at Cambridge last spring, thinking I'd be back there by now. Instead, I wear two parkas, one over the other.

Any progress I've made in raising support for my prediction that the next big shift in the outdoor industry will be toward the 'hermit market' is invisible. The gear manufacturers are still years away from developing new products aimed specifically at new hermits. My work is cut out for me. Stacy Bare and I have had a few conversations during which we touched on the subject. Stacy is a veteran of the Afghanistan War, who on returning, self-medicated his PTSD first with drugs and alcohol and then wildness. We met over our common interest in 'awe.' Where my interest is in the relationship between experiencing awe and our pro-social behavior, Stacy is showing it to be an antidote to PTSD for veterans. Stacy is young and strong and carries an XXL heart in his chest. He once suggested we write together about "Stoke" vs. "Awe" in the outdoor experience. "Stoke" refers to the adrenaline-produced thrill and excitement associated with the extreme dimension of the outdoor experience. 'Stoke' pays the bills: company-sponsored young people developing their bodies to put them faster into higher, farther, steeper, and more dangerous places, which with Instagram and YouTube are instantly converted (reduced) to playgrounds or stages on which truly spectacular feats are acted out. But would photos of a hermit in a blue puffy Patagonia "Fitzroy" parka watching the cold desert light change sell many? Probably not.

Still I believe that spending any time in the wilds makes one a better person, but there are variables. Yes, Keltner et al., have proven scientifically that experiencing awe contributes to 'pro-social' behaviors—the desire to contribute to the greater good. But I've also learned that experiencing 'awe' in unlikely during exposure to emotional or physical danger. While there are extreme athletes who are emotionally, physically, and financially committed to 'pro-social' causes (especially causes which directly impact their professions, such as climate and wilderness protection), the two are not necessarily aligned. I am convinced that *contemplative* time in the wilds is more conducive to 'awe' and the 'pro-social behavior' that accompanies it.

How then, I wonder sitting here, contemplatively, hoping to shorten the long night by staying upright as long as possible, *are Hermits impacted by awe?*

Hermits like wilderness more than civilization. Hermits seek contemplation and solitude in the wilderness, which opens them to awe. Which is why hermits pursue the greater good, and why hermits are perceived to be wise and sought out for their wisdom.

Again, this may be due to my age, but the hermit dimension of the wild world seems worth considering for its potential good. This could be the 'hermit tradition' that America lacks.

Perhaps we divide our parks and wild places into sacrifice zones and sacred zones. Both *words have "sac"*[8] *as its root.* This implies that what is sacrificed can't be sacred. "Sacrifice" means giving up something for a higher purpose. National Parks are spectacular natural landscapes that multitudes want to experience. Accommodating growing numbers of visitors means sacrificing wildness. The higher purpose for which wildness is sacrificed is that society benefits in proportion to the numbers of its members who experience natural wonders.

The sacrifice zones are like most of Arches and Yosemite National Parks, which are designed to provide comfort and education to large numbers of people.

"Sacred zones" would be for hermits. Hermits would need solitude for contemplation. Few facilities would be necessary in 'Sacred Zones.' Camping would be low impact. Some areas would require quotas and permits. "Sacred Zones" would be for those seeking an 'existential', awe-inducing experience. In defining 'wilderness,' The Wilderness Act itself comes close to describing 'Sacred Zones.'"

Where a 'sacrifice zone' provides the outer world experience, the 'sacred zone' encourages the traveler's inner world experience.

Years ago, while exploring the notion that tourism may have a role in changing the world, I came across the word "existential" in *Spiritual Tourism: Travel and Religious Practice in Western Society*,[9] a book by Alex Norman, an Australian scholar. The book categorizes tourists according to relationship to their 'center.' I knew the word *existential* when I saw it but had never seen *or imagined it* in the context of 'tourism.' According to the book, tourist/travelers have one of five possible experiences, including *recreational, experiential, experimental,* and *existential, and diversional*— those who travel to temporarily escape regimented and pressurized modern lives. 'Existential' tourists—*also referred to as 'pilgrims'*—travel as a spiritual practice to access places of higher meaning. They're dedicated to collective well-being. That five different people could be in the same physical place at the same time and have these five different experiences fascinates me. Perhaps there's a sixth tourist experience—the *Hermit tourist.*

The complete wall of darkness approaches from just beyond the reach of my firelight, the beginning of a long night. Sitting here, time seems to have come to a complete stop. Sleeping on the ground always takes some getting used to. That, and the long winter night will mean a continuous series of short naps until morning.

My eyes fight to stay open, and my stick pile shrinks beyond my reach. I turn off my headlamp and feel the darkness move in around me, overwhelming the fire as it dies. Whatever anxiousness I had confronting a long cold night softens into wondering about what the darkness will hold.

The fire is now a small pile of glowing jewels. I extricate myself from my seat and wander over to my sleeping bag. The moon just appeared, and around it a vivid ring announcing the upcoming storm.

I sleep fitfully, dreaming shallow unremembered dreams while asleep and watching the clouds while awake. Concentric rings of clouds partially surround the moon like a heavenly wreath. Stars come and go with the clouds that swirl in a great high wind which I cannot hear or feel. Another 'nap' and then awake to long thin clouds shifting in the sky, the night gauzy, unsettled.

I wake from my fourth nap in complete clarity and pure darkness but for the Milky Way glimmering with such brightness that all other stars fade toward black. Given wings, I would follow it anywhere.

If I dream at all, my dreams are short and scattered and more of a nuisance than anything. Now, near the middle of the night, a dream comes back to me from the early days of the pandemic.

The dream itself was simple: *Siamese twins, Men conjoined at the sides of their heads, two bodies but one brain. The dream was a rehash of their life, including the lead man, his controlling personality, his university frat boy life, the two of them growing older and responsible together, one aggressive and successful, the other more contemplative. Then, tired of being led around, the quiet one kills the other separating himself from his brother and taking the one brain they had shared. In the final scene the living brother holds a bloody knife, the side of his own head, a mangled mess. He knew that he had risked his own life, but he needed freedom*

Two different masculine sides of myself, with one brain which could not be divided. Two different but identical bodies. Two aging masculine bodies. One breaks loose, killing the other (one part of my masculine dies, killed by the other), the other one, wounded, possibly having sacrificed his life for his freedom. I told my dream to Terry, who saw the impact. "You should call Susan," she said, referring to a friend in Cambridge, a Jungian psychologist.

"People are dreaming again," Susan told me, referring to what she was noticing as one of the pandemic's many impacts.

She asked me to tell her the dream slowly. She asked a few questions and then suggested that it may be 'Biblical'—Cain and Abel, which I loved. Most important was her advice to keep after it, to keep it in my mind and watch it as it continuously unfolds, opens up.

Out walking the afternoon following my phone call with Susan, something amazing happened. I'm always on the lookout for small reddish stone flakes with perfect white circles, which may be the fossil remnant of an ancient plant. I collect the smallest ones I find. I love the white on red contrast and the perfection of the circle. I was moving quickly along a trail I'd been on thirty times, when there beneath me was a small red flake with not one perfect white circle, but two. Conjoined.

I went through periods throughout the summer, wondering which if any of my close men friends might represent my now separated brother. (None). I considered the possibility that my younger brother might be the 'brother I'd killed in the dream to free myself. Symbolically, of course.

Joey and I are two years apart in age and much further than that in philosophy. He and his wife, Jann, have four kids and a quiver of grandkids. He's just retired after selling the family business. He's always been a frugal entrepreneur—going back to when we were kids, and he would buy candy bars for a nickel and sell them for a quarter two days into a weeklong scout trip. He's very conservative, and the one time we talked serious politics was not pretty. He's a great family man and friend. He's a stalwart in the Mormon Church and a lot of fun to be around. He's not my dream's separated twin for two obvious reasons:

we never have and would never share a brain, and he's too intelligent to have had his brain removed.

There's a third reason. Dreams are personal. My Siamese twin dream is not about me and another person, but about two different sides of myself.

That dream has reignited, and I'm wide awake, the stars and clouds pressing down upon me. The twins are back, the lead twin—the masculine fraternity boy side of me, the 'me' who was all that is expected of men coming of age, the 'me' that is patriarchy, being hacked away by the other twin, who keeps the brain, free at last. *My twin is not dead. He's out there moving around in the world without a brain.* He's bleeding profusely. He—the Patriarchy severed from its brain—cannot survive, will soon die. I sit upright. I take two deep breaths.

The white patriarchy is not thinking clearly, about the coronavirus or climate collapse—or anything that matters to anyone who believes in collective compassion. They will not listen to scientists or doctors. They pay no attention to what occurs in the realm of dreams.

My bladder wakes me up, dawn still off in the invisible distance. I'm the dragonfly extracting myself from my nymph shell in which I've been encased, developing, transforming— and struggle to my feet in the darkness. A bit off balance, I step from my sleeping bag onto the Earth. How soft the ground feels on my bare feet, and less cold than expected. I walk gingerly toward the edge of my space, each step expecting to feel a painful stab by a sharp stone. The airy, soft sand absorbs anything hard that I step on, and I think about walking around a bit on the cloud-soft surface, but don't. It's colder than I think.

Peeing into the darkness, I sense the presence of TIP, (Trump's in Office), my first demon. My demons have not been regular visitors. Like so many Americans, I've grown so used to Trump's lies and narcissistic antics that TIP has lost most of his power. What remains dissipates with my wakefulness and disappears into the shadows.

Back in my bag, staring up, the heavens are alive, dancing and jumping and floating above me. YATT, "You are Totally Toast" —the demon who reminds me of the worst possible physical scenario I could face—is nowhere to be found. Looking ahead, my safe passage into whatever's next is clear and safe.

I'd not heard from or seen LISBB, "Life is Still Beautiful, But…." for ages. LISBB's absence may be due to my changing attitude, that regardless of my personal situation, or the situation of America or the world, Life is not "still beautiful' as if that beauty is fleeting. And no 'But's' because, with pure beauty, there are no exceptions. LISBB only demonized me until I realized that beauty is not optional, that it can never disappear, except in my own life when I refuse to see it. But, and this is a huge, "but," I acknowledge the privilege I have which allows me to see and know this. And the corresponding question: how best do I spread my privilege?

Which leaves, WHID.

My "What Have I Done With My Life" demon, always seems to be lurking nearby. At my age, or at some certain point in life, one must accept what one is, what one has become, and like it or not, realize that "This" now is what I've done with my life.

I am lucky. I cannot help what I have. I face a simple choice: do I spend my energy, creativity protecting all that I have, celebrate my privilege, and use it to measure my importance in the world? Or do I use the privilege I'm lucky enough to have contributing to more balance on the planet?

I was in Maine teaching during my father's lasts days and his death. This didn't bother me, as although we didn't agree on many things, we had no unfinished business. While passing through Salt Lake City getting from Castle Valley to Cambridge the previous summer and fall, I'd stayed with him for days at a time. We were like two old bachelors—"is that old meat or new cheese?"—going for walks, cooking together. He'd told me on occasion that we needed to have "a little chat" about the Mormon Church—I knew that he wondered why his own son rejected what he'd dedicated his entire life to. We never got around to it.

We talked on the phone often. Here's how one call ended: "Oh, and I've got a bone to pick with you," he said, which worried me a bit. "You used the "F" word on Facebook," He said. He said, "I didn't teach you that!".

"You didn't teach me what a mess this country would be, either," I said.

"True there," he said.

"I didn't know you looked at Facebook," I said.

"How else would I keep track of all of you? Thanks for the call. I love you."

"I love you."

I'd been in Maine a week when Terry called to tell me that he was in the hospital, in and out of consciousness, and while conscious, he was off in some far-away place. There were decisions and conversations among my siblings and I on Facetime. The last time I talked to him, I told him I loved him and missed him and that my classes were going well. He didn't respond much. Then, I said, "Dad, I'm not sure what happens to us when we die, where we go. When you get over there, please send me a signal, something to let me know that there is something out there and that you've arrived." He had a finger clip that measured his oxygen levels with a red light on it. Due to Facetime and bandwidth and distance, the red light was blurred, and looked like ET's green, lit up finger in Steven Spielberg's movie. He raised his hand and twirled it above him, the red light on his finger spinning around in circles. He spiraled his hand up until the red light shown at the end of his outstretched arm. All the while, he mumbled words I could not understand. Then he went quiet. "I love you, dad," I said for the last time. He died two days later.

Class was tough the day following his death. Late that afternoon, I noticed that thousands of dark birds had convened in trees surrounding the house where I was living, sharply contrasted against the gray cloudy skies. When I opened the door to watch, the birds took to the sky in one huge moment and swirled around the house and spiraled in expanding circles above me. I knew that this was the same swirling and spiraling my father had done with his hand with its lit-up fingertip. This was his signal. He'd arrived somewhere. Part of him was out there.

I saw a fascinating map recently showing ocean and dry land in proper proportions. The world maps we've all grown up with show the continents and countries holding all the people of the world made up most of the Earth's surface, surrounded by areas of blue water. This 'map of the planet if you are a fish' took on a different meaning. I saw the oceans as deep time and evolutionary history, and infinite possibility. Poking periodically up through the liquid blue mass, landforms represent our conscious modern lives, lives of reason and thought. Oceans, I discovered, make up 70% of our planet.

While I doubt the accuracy of this metaphor, seeing pictorially the land as conscious material as a small fraction of the whole, compared to the ocean representing the unconscious, helps me. The blue in the picture in my mind represents the information to which modernity denied us access, but also the massive potential once we learn to dive and swim.

Wide awake after rolling off my pillow face-first into the cool sand, I look around at the quiet. I sit up and see the radius of my vision expand as I rise above it. I love that book, "The Powers of Ten," which is a series of photographs of a couple picnicking in a park, each taken from a level below the one before it, beginning many light years out in the universe. Each photo moves closer by a 'power of ten' until the earth comes into view, then the continents, North America, the park, the picnicking people. I imagine similar photographs taken of my camp. In my half-conscious state, I watch a film as the camera drops closer and closer and there it is, my sleeping bag the tiny blue dot surrounded by a sand layer, capped by stone, cut by canyons, the only indication of my camp. I sense a pressure, a compression, a force contained within the borders of each photo, which have taken on a third dimension. Lower down this force thickens, and the pressure mounts. There I am, the camera close enough to recognize myself, inside my small cube. I feel personal security but also great restriction and high tension. Higher, in a bigger and bigger cube, yes, with less security and tension, but more freedom. Regardless of the vantage, I am huddled and warm. As the camera flies back toward the stars, my blue dot existence disappears, but my entire Pandemic Universe fills my vision. At home, in my cube (a room, our house), the pressure is great, as is the tension. I am obsessed with the news, which I take personally. I've seen the past four years as an assault on what I hold dear, on my work. Outside in a wild and much larger cube, I am not alone. The camera now high in the stars, and me in a cube big enough to include the solar system and beyond. I share my angst with millions. Trump coming to power is not a unique or separate story, but part of the long story which began in the deep past and will continue into the distant invisible future.

At this point in the long story, a deadly organism is sent to earth to cleanse it by destroying life. But not all life, only human life. A virus. The latest hope to eliminate the scourge that has fouled the air and water killed off other life at alarming rates, and warmed the atmosphere with fatal greenhouse gases. Clear it all away, like poisoning a lake to rid it of a destructive invasive species. (Humans have become the worst invasive species). And not all humans, only the half that came from afar, living on the ancient spore, by their own set of rules and the belief that they deserve whatever they can take. The other half, immune.

Paul Hawken wrote, "The social justice movement, the environmental movement, and indigenous movements are intertwining, morphing, and becoming the largest social movement in the history of the world. Humanity's IMMUNE response to political corruption, economic disease, and environmental degradation."[10] He conceived this not as ideology but by separating what is humane from what is not, termed it humanity's collective immune system

The people comprising *humanity's immune system* are part of the same faction of Americans believing that wearing masks is key to controlling the Hermit Virus, which otherwise could not select who it infects and who it does not. Masks also minimize the amount of the spore we inhale.

We absorbed Trump into our consciousness as the symbol of American White Supremacy. Like an invasive species, White Supremacy is a monoculture destroying natural diversity.

Long before WWII, Jung had a dream[11] predicting the war and the Nazis, but also that.".... *as the Christian view of the world loses its authority, the more menacingly will the 'blond beast' be heard prowling about in its underground prison, ready at any moment to burst out with devastating consequences.*" That the dream included the term "Blond Beast" makes me shudder.

Powerful white American men driven by the Spore in its late stage believe that by climbing the grass stalk, they elevate themselves above "other", and become evolution's crowning glory. Instead, the top of the tallest blade of grass is where they will die right before the mushroom erupts from their head.

Wide awake, as if a balloon has popped next to my head. I've been asleep, for how long I don't have a clue, but dreamlessly. WHID ("What have I done with my life?") is back reminding me again that my 'one story' (*our living in Pleistocene, evolutionary bodies, our having problems because we're living in a world vastly different from the one we were designed for*) might be the WRONG *fucking story.*[12] My demons know this is a way to get to me, to distract and confuse me and while I feel ready for this question when it arrives, it always upsets me. It *has* to be the right story. If it is the wrong story, then I would need to abandon decades of thinking and writing and being, something I'm unwilling to do. I have, however, watched my 'one story' grow and change. The change lately has been to realize that we don't have much hope if biological evolution is our only option— it's too slow. However, evolution is necessary as we've reached a point where the antics of modern humans—the technologies we've developed, along with the superior attitudes about wealth and power—seriously threaten not just our own future but that of life on earth. My demon wants me to doubt my story, to believe it has become obsolete.

Climate change.

Laying under the stars trying to quiet my mind to sleep, I'm surprised by the thoughts that have waited to fill any vacuum that forms. The value of my demons may be in how they force me to think further. My 'one story' may be obsolete in that my use of the word "Pleistocene" in relation to evolution assumes 'biological' evolution. Biological evolution has not significantly changed our bodies in the 200,000 years since we emerged during the Pleistocene on our own twig of the Tree of Life. We have been altering the climate by burning fossil carbon for power for 200 years. Biological evolution has been working on us for 10,000 generations (figuring 20 years per generation), but our modern technologies, and numbers, and lifestyles have disrupted the climate for a scant ten generations. At this pace, biological evolution can't possibly keep up. Not so with *conscious* evolution. Global Warming/climate disruption is a *changing condition* to which life must adapt or die. We've known it was coming. We may not have known the speed at which it was coming. We could not have imagined the political ineptitude and arrogance which has quickened it. We are conscious of climate change. Therefore we must adapt consciously.

Unlike four years ago, I've seen no signs of life. Then, besides a moth and various flies, I saw many tracks—deer, small rodents, and that wild cat, which caused me some concern. I'm in the same place at the same time as before. The recent snowstorm may have been the difference. Or, the difference may be another example of recent climate-related trends—the megadrought. Reports[13] published this past year tell of a drought gripping the southwestern U.S., which, based on tree-ring data, is the worst in 500 years. In the past natural variations caused by, say, a temporary rise in the temperature of the Pacific Ocean were responsible for these droughts. Now, models show that anthropogenic climate change accounts for nearly half of this drought's severity.

Summer was hot with no real rain. The river was low, and remains so. In September, I dug holes to plant trees and, down two feet, found more dust than dirt. Friends down valley who irrigate notice drastic diminishment of surface water. River runoff comes earlier due to dust blown from here covering the Colorado Mountains giving the snow a red tint which quickens its melting. The average temperature rise in our county has already surpassed the maximum determined at the Paris Climate Accords. We have a well, which seems okay, for now. The deer who spend winter and spring in the valley seem healthy. Except one, who until a few days ago would limp by a few times each week, drooling. We hear coyotes less often.

Here, the juniper trees look good. Cliffrose have retreated, leaving their outermost twigs leaf-bare. The white alkali cliff stains which seem to grow with drought, are huge. I've seen no birds: No Juncos or Spotted Towhees, and none of the common sparrows who should be picking seeds from the base of plants. Only ravens with their vast territories.

For years we've been hearing that based on the current loss of species we're experiencing, we're seeing the Sixth major extinction of life on earth. This has been corrected. This is not the Sixth Extinction, but the First Extermination.[14]

This is not cyclical. This is the trend. We are altering the rhythms of nature, breaking the cycles. With climate change, change is forever. The changes are the new conditions on which evolution is working. This terrifying loss of life impacts everything and everyone everywhere in visible and invisible ways.

Half asleep, I'm aware of my right ear, on which I'm lying. I chuckle, realizing that I'm not wearing my Hermit Virus mask held by rubber bands around my ears. I'm definitely 'socially distant.' Six feet? No, I'm miles from anyone. Peter and Anne are asleep in their home on the Professor Valley Ranch miles away as the raven flies. To the east, nothing all the way to Colorado. Our home would be the nearest in Castle Valley, three miles away. And somewhere within two miles from here, climbers are likely camped, waiting to climb. Besides being my most preferred location, the middle of nowhere is free of the Hermit Virus.

My mind hops image to image, as if rock to rock across a stream I must cross, getting from here to there. My ears holding my mask to the maskless hoards at MAGA rallies believing the Hermit Virus is a hoax, and then coming screeching to a halt at recent conversations I've heard second hand from people I trust. An "angry white man" told one friend that the "only option left is to kill the liberals," and another, " it will be like hunting."

From there, I step not too far to the image of our 'son' Louis during Rwandan Genocide in 1994 and all we learned about that horrid history. How different is our current divide from that separating the Hutus and Tutsis in Rwanda? How similar? Or between the Nazis and Jews leading to the Holocaust. Or tens of millions killed for their stature, belief, or race, at other times in a dozen other places. Our own Civil War.

Humans have endured terrible things. These periods of massive loss of human life seem to "pulse" through time, are rhythmic, cyclic. We look back, hoping that knowing this dark history means not needing to repeat it. But then, repeat, we do. Over and over. Why would we be immune? But then "this is different".

My shallow breathing and increased heart rate indicate the presence of Demon YATT (You are Totally Toast), suggesting the remote possibility that during my absence, Biden has become our next president, which has incited violence, perhaps close to home. I've been scared to death of possible post-election violence. Recall Michael Caputo, Trump's assistant secretary of public affairs at the Department of Health and Human Services. After trying to manipulate the scientists at the CDC into creating pro-Trump Covid reports, Caputo went a little nuts in a video he put on social media prompting his people to buy ammunition for the fights sure to come when Trump doesn't step aside at Biden's inauguration. Later, Caputo went onto say that his own "mental health has definitely failed."

Remember *Catch 22*? In this famous novel, Joseph Heller coined the phrase which has come to mean "a dilemma or difficult circumstance from which there is no escape because of mutually conflicting or dependent conditions."

The actual situation from which the term "Catch 22" arose was more specific. Yossarian, the main character, believes that if he feigns insanity, he won't be sent on more dangerous bombing missions. But, because of his desire not to throw himself into danger, he can't possibly be insane.

That Caputo refers to his failing mental health scares me, begging the question, *is someone who addresses his own deteriorating mental health, healthier mentally than someone who cannot and will not acknowledge it?*

That's one thing. The other is that Caputo is saying that his current situation is affecting him mentally. And again, at least he admits it. How about all those people who are so obviously losing it mentally but have no clue. All the lying and deception Trump forces his people to do must erode their mental health. Caputo might have known something about the upcoming elections that he could not personally accommodate—morally or mentally—and was calling out for help.

The spore. Bursting from his head.

Another 'pulse' in the deadly rhythm of the world.

That would be optimistic. This current situation is not a pulse, not just a different terrible throb in history. We're seeing the rotting core of capitalism and democracy threatened. But worse, we're witnessing in real-time as climate collapse alters the rhythms and cycles of life itself.

A throb would suggest that once Trump goes—either now or in another four years, the country will go back to 'normal.' This assumes that 'normal' is acceptable, which it is not. "Normal" is the path toward our own destruction. Granted Trump changed that path, making it more direct, taking a shortcut, with more velocity toward our own extinction.

"Extinction is the rule," Carl Sagan once said. "Survival is the exception."

How strange that had the Coronavirus not flooded the world when it did, Trump's re-election might not be in doubt.

I am stuck, spinning around and around. The demons affect me mentally, but also physically, as if they infect my blood with something dark and sticky, and I cannot move. I recognize the feeling. The "hermit" in me seeks wisdom and understanding, and immunity from the demons. But I cannot move. WHID is back, with a slightly different question. "*What if their story is right?*"

Enough. I am fully awake and see this for what it is. Any story that abandons the deep story of how we, one species among many, got this far cannot be right.

I shake my head in my sleeping bag. WHID and I have been here before. If by 'their' story, he (I'm sure WHID is male) means my family's story, the Mormon, religious story. I can't ignore how five generations of influence can linger.

"How could that story be right?" I rhetorically ask myself out loud. If I'd ever questioned myself for leaving the Mormon Church, I will never again. Too many individual members swear their undying support for Trump—that weak symbol of a man who has lived his entire life according to principles so diametrically opposed to those I had drilled into me as a Mormon boy.

Some—but by no means, all—traditional Mormons began expressing their displeasure with Trump in the lead-up to the 2016 Presidential election. His despicable behavior—lying, cheating, immorality—contributed to a vision that made me wonder how anyone considering themselves a "good Mormon" could support this man for American's highest office. Trump's character, plus the old adage that one cannot be both a good Mormon and a Democrat, opened up enough space for a Third Party candidate, Evan McMullin, an ex-CIA business executive.

Although many of our family members voted for McMullin in 2016, he came in third.[15] Trump, who grabs pussy, mocks disabled people, cheats, lies, and is probably a Russian asset, is, after all, a Republican. He did garner the fewest Utah votes of any recent Republican candidate in recent history but still won the state.

While details of his atrocious behaviors mount, Trump still has many Utahans—Mormons—under his spell. During a private conversation a year into the Trump administration, a well-known Mormon leader, when asked what he thought of Trump, said, "He's a bit rough around the edges, but he's giving us what we want."

'What we want'. Aside from stricter abortion laws, this may refer to propping up the carbon industry, which is seen as a boon to rural Utah communities, and deregulating financial institutions. Financial regulations may inhibit some of the schemes by which Mormons cheat their trusting ward members.

In other words, Trump is 'useful,' regardless of who he is with his immoral and unlawful character. I love Cormac McCarthy's book, *All the Pretty Horses*. I've memorized a number of passages. In one scene, the main character has fallen in love with a young woman in Mexico. Her grandmother says this about her: "I only know that if she does not come to value what is true above what is useful, it will make little difference whether she lives at all."

What is true? What is useful?

That term, "useful." Laying here in the dark, my face exposed to the cold clear night as I stare up into it, I see "useful" in *its full* destructive power. Lately, *useful* seems to have replaced 'truth.' Somewhere along the way, we've lost the idea of 'truth' as a standard, by which we decide between things.

We've witnessed how Trump's addiction to wealth and power has made truth his great enemy. It also makes him *useful* to any person, group, or corporation who might use him to amass more of their own wealth and power. I imagined that early on, he sat down and made this list of the major groups or industries whose support he needed and who might benefit from his position as POTUS.

The evangelicals would overlook everything else about him if he were strongly 'pro-life.' The white supremacists knew he was one of them, that he would be hard on migration and soft on police brutality against People of Color. The carbon industry needed a shot in the arm to keep going—less regulation and environmental protection—even though it is on its last legs. The Gun lobby could not afford any regulation whatsoever. The financial industry needed lower taxes and less regulation. The War Machine needed a hawk as president, and new wars, or the hope for new wars.

Then he negotiated. Quid Pro Quo. This for that.

Photos embedded in my mind from Trump's visit to Utah in January of 2018 flash in front of me. He was with Mormon leaders touring the Church Welfare Center. Later that day, he would cut the Grand Staircase/Escalante National Monument in half and slash Bears Ears by 85%, to a shadow of its former self. I wonder what phone calls occurred between Trump and Mormon Republican leaders prior to that. "Get your people behind me, and I'll deal with those monuments," I imagine Trump saying. No doubt that Trump's growing support among Utah Republicans between the two elections had a great deal to do with his National Monument actions—how useful he'd become. This negated the fact that the truth of his life was anti-thetical to anything remotely close to what Mormons believe or how they're to act and live.

I imagine Utah Republicans—all Republicans?—getting a daily memo prepared by those who are really in power—the corporations. The memo I see has talking points and exact quotes for politicians to use in dealing with an issue. These memos are specific to each politician as they wouldn't all want to sound the same. These memos also remind the politicians not to heed any criticism coming from the populous, because we the people are like pesky flies who only become peskier if attention is paid to us. The Corporations laugh at us. They know that if they spend enough money wooing us around elec-tion time, they will control the outcome. That's been the story up to now.

Another image rises in front of me: that baby-Trump balloon flying over London. Since first hearing the phrase, "Corporate Personhood," I've pictured the 'corporate person' as a horny young boy who thinks about nothing but satisfying his own prurient desires, elevating his own worth, never looking at the consequences. I knew when I saw that balloon exactly who the 'person' who is "corporate person-hood" is.

The demons do not destroy my calm. They only mask it. They are quiet now.

While the calm I've grown over the past four years is based on getting better at accepting the inevitable, part of it is a deepening understanding of "Truth." Growing up in the Mormon Church, I was told that the only "truth" was what which was revealed to *our* prophet. Our truth was truer than Catholic or Protestant truth or any other truth. That worked briefly until I stepped outside, beyond it all, where *wildness* became pure 'truth.' I realized that by any other standard, most "truth" was filtered through belief. But one truth can't argue with another truth unless both are less than pure truths. Something is "true" if it supports, encourages, and affirms life. Biology. Biology, the science of life. Biological truth is the truth of life. Evolutionary Biology is the subfield of biology looking into the evolutionary forces responsible for the diversity of life on Earth, including our own direct connection to the pure origin of life. In the 19th Century, Charles Darwin described this in his writings about natural selection, including *The Origin of Species* and *The Descent of Man.*

I'm comforted thinking that Lao Tzu may have been writing about evolutionary biology 2500 years before Darwin. His book, *The Tao de Ching*, describes "the Way," which refers to the Tao. Taoists consider "the Way" as the intuitive knowledge of the natural order of things.[16] The Tao is fundamental. It does two things: it observes what is, and it states what tends to happen when an animal goes against its own way, acts in opposition to its biology. Going against its biology can lead to the death of the individual animal and the extinction of the species. From the *Tao de Ching*, Chapter 30, "That which goes against the Tao

comes to an early end" Or "what's not the way soon ends." The
Tao and biology have no preferences—no 'should's' or 'ought's.'
The Tao, the "Way," like biology applies across the full spectrum
of life. It does not give a pass to even the most powerful and
wealthy white men. We are all animals. We are all subject to the
same forces. Much of what happens these days is "not the way."
The Tao—biology—is the most basic truth. Pure truth.

If biology is the natural order of life, physics is the natural
order of the universe. In his book, *The Tao of Physics,*[17] Fritjof
Capra shows that an "essential harmony" exists between western science and Eastern wisdom. He notes that in the west,
we've limited our view of physics to its technological, mecha-
nistic, *most useful* form. In fact, he says, modern physics goes
far beyond technology, that the "Way" or "Tao" of physics
"can be a path with a heart, a way to spiritual knowledge and
self-realization."

Friends who spend time in the wilds inherently understand
this concept of pure truth. Today's Republicans give this truth
no consideration, and seem to do whatever they can to unravel
it, which is unraveling life itself. We must change the story. We
can no longer elect officials whose policies support death, not
life. We need leaders who love all life—not just White American
lives— and who seek pure biological, evolutionary truth.

Here, in Utah, our Mormon Leaders are in this anti-life
lockstep. They support their party in heaping suffering upon
migrant families at the border, cutting taxes of the most wealthy
1% of Americans, exploding the national debt which will be
paid for by the 99% forever, opposing any gun regulation, doing

irreparable damage to the planet with deregulation, and refusing to acknowledge America's role in the warming climate when
the long-predicted signs (fire, record warm temperatures, rising
seas) are appearing like clockwork. This justifies my abandon-
ing religion years ago.

Did I misread the scriptures? Do they actually say, "Do
unto other straight white Euro-Americans as you would have
other straight white Euro-Americans do unto you?" Did Jesus
really say, "Love your straight White Euro-American neighbors as yourself?" And you call yourselves 'pro-life,' saying that
'abortion is the deal breaker.' No. You may be 'pro' white-Eu-
ro-American lives, unborn lives. You are not 'pro' my life. You
are not 'pro' the life of any person of color, indigenous person.
You are certainly not 'pro' more-than-human life. You are not
really 'pro' life. This is the ultimate hypocrisy, which must be
some kind of evil.[18] "Serious spore infestation" is the only way
this makes sense.

I feel safe here, camped in a far corner of Grand County, one
of only three of Utah's 29 counties to choose Biden, who lost in
Utah by more than 20%.

There are a number of reasons I might be laying out here in
the dirt, in the early winter, staring up at the night sky. I could
be here for an excuse, an escape from reality, which is how reasonable members of society might view it. Or, I could be using
time in the wilderness to better understand civilization, which
is how I view it. And, I trust there's a deeper reason I'm not
conscious of. The theory exists[19] that of all people who have

ever lived, only 2% traveled more than 50 miles from where they were born, motivated by a unique brain allele to explore and seek reward. Long, long ago, this allele in the brains of a few of our earliest ancestors had survival implications. When food became scarce, one of our group, motivated by the allele, had wandered off to explore and found new food sources. I might have this condition.

There's that. But then there's this: I descend from those 85,000 Mormons who emigrated to Utah from Europe in the mid to late nineteenth century—far, far more than "50 miles from where they were born". The Mormon Migration is often cited as one of the great stories of Manifest Destiny, that long, fateful period in history that began in Europe with the rumor of America being God's chosen place. White Europeans were encouraged to move there, suppress the wilderness, overcome the native people, and take advantage of all the natural wealth existing there. Oh, and wait for God. All Euro-Americans descend from people who, for various reasons, left their homes and traveled many more than 50 miles. Therefore, this allele must exist here in a much higher percentage, which helps explain our ability to focus on and become obsessed with, unlimited rewards. Perhaps this allele has mutated into the "Spore."

Dizzy from my mind spinning inside my head, I feel as if I've slept for the last time, ever, that I will never ever sleep again. Knowing logically that this isn't true, I relax. Instead of burrowing deeper into my sleeping bag, I stare out. I recall being 'eager' rather than 'anxious' about what was sure to be many dark, sleepless hours. I stare up into the darkness and think about the effect watching the starry night had on the consciousness of our ancestors throughout our deep history.

Whether or not we're conscious of it, we long for basic, bedrock truth. For ancient truth. The truth that our earliest ancestors relied on for basic survival. Much of this truth came at night, once the cooking fire had turned to embers, and we looked up into the night. What information, insight, inspiration did we find there? This same information that contributed to our survival for ten thousand generations is still available to some of us.

Although this thought is not new to me, once I realize that sleep will be rare if non-existent state, my "night work" begins. My world has expanded to include not just ordinary everyday reality but also the inner deep un-worded truths lurking in my unconscious. My night work is as important as my day job. My *"Night work" happens in my unconscious.*

This all solidified for me a year ago. I was driving to Cambridge after attending an inspiring climate rally at Colby College during which Ed Abbey and others, considered heroic by many, were again outed for their misogynist and racist behavior. Again, I was feeling conflicted about Abbey's bad behavior while acknowledging the positive role he's played in my life. I saw a highway construction sign flashing, "Night work starts, Sept 22nd" the same basic sign I'd seen years before in New Hampshire. To Abbey, "night work" was the work he did at night—to literally dismantle earth-destroying machines. Clearly, my 'night work' is also necessary to dismantle anything that might otherwise destroy the Earth.

My night work is very clear: stare out at the stars while awake; dream while asleep.

Due to light pollution, only ten percent of the world's population can see the Milky Way. Mostly invisible now are the constellations and the stories of birth and death, light and dark, magic and gods and goddesses, they tell. During the Hermit Virus, we've made a habit of watching the night sky—Castle Valley is a great place for darkness, as even outdoor lighting is regulated to enhance it. We spent July nights sitting on the porch waiting in the dimming of the day's last light for the Neowise comet to appear in the northern sky.

Since first learning about 'awe' I've realized how often I associate awe with looking up into the dark night sky. Those nights watching Neowise were filled with awe. Seeing Neowise required a dark sky. Neowise provoked awe. Much of the world could not see Neowise because of too much light and too many tall buildings. How many "people in power" saw Neowise during the summer? Or how many corporate heads or National politicians even heard about it, or are ever anywhere dark enough to view the night sky? Or, ever experienced awe like that found staring at the night sky?

Awe seems absent in any form from public dialogue these days. Many times I've said to myself, "These people all need to get out more," referring to the wilds, which I believe to be the foundation for all truth. "Awe" in any of its true forms, seems never to pierce the thickening veneer that most politicians, all Republicans, seem to move around within, a casing that protects them from actual life.

Dachar Keltner, my "awe mentor," writes that 'awe' *shrinks* the 'self' causing us to focus beyond ourselves to the collective good. In another of his books, *The Paradox of Power*, Keltner writes that power *expands* the self. The more power people get, the less they care about their social environment and the more about their personal desires. "Awe" contributes to 'pro-social behaviors,' power becomes 'anti-social.' People in power are less likely to experience awe. This is a problem.

The Jewish theologian Abraham Joshua Heschel said that "wisdom" is fostered by "awe."[20]

No awe, no insight. No wisdom. Then, the amount of power (or wealth) one has is inversely proportional to one's wisdom and insight. Our current political problem begins to make sense. Making sense of a problem is the first step in solving it.

"Wisdom" is a tricky word.

The cliffs above me are suddenly visible, bathed in peach light. I've slept through the transition to dawn. The cloud filter purples the sky, "Provincial" (6B11) or possibly "Daydream" (6E4), according to my cyanometer. I'll go with "Daydream."

Based on how stiff I am, I've been asleep or trying to sleep for twelve hours. Slowly I raise myself into a sitting position and keeping my sleeping bag pulled around me, I look around, eager to see what night has done to my world. Sunrise filtered through thickened clouds turns the eastern sky red. The intermittent breeze becomes constant and thick and carries the organic and sweet scent of a nearby storm.

The wind makes no sound until it encounters something: an opening in the rocks; the cliff edge as it passes over; stiff branches which vibrate but do not bend. The wind across the canyon makes a sweeping sound as it moves low among the cliffs. This sound is different from the 'hum' I always hear, audible beneath the silence. I regularly hear this hum at home and often wonder what it is. I've read about a 'hum' in other deserts in New Mexico near Taos, which disturbed many of the residents there. For me, the hum is 'presence,' and I hear it only in the 'absence' of all other sounds.

Pink turns to orange, which migrates down the cliff in front of me.

For those early hermits, the early religious ascetics who planted the seeds for most modern religion, the desert provided the scarcity and silence they needed to fast and pray and be near God. Thomas Merton, the great writer/hermit/mystic, wrote many books that are important to me. In one, *The Wisdom of the Desert*, Merton uses their own quotes to illustrate the lives of early Christian desert mystics. I liked the book, especially Merton's introduction.[21] At first, the content confused me. While the 'wisdom' was there, ever-present, the desert was missing. No descriptions, no metaphors, no views or sunsets or night skies. No animals or plants. Not a fly or beetle, ant, or smell. I've never visited those specific deep African deserts, but I know they cannot be completely featureless lifeless plains. Those early hermits wanted only 'absence,' believing that without the obstacles present in everyday life, God could enter in. Where no sound exists, there is silence. Where one has no possessions, there is scarcity. Many early hermits believed that the more they suffered, the more likely they would meet god.

In contrast, for the Chinese Hermits, the wilderness was 'presence.' Many of their poems have survived to be read over and over again throughout the centuries since they were written. The wild world is a constant presence in their poems. Nature was their source of meaning and understanding of the world. I've memorized this by Tao Yuanming, 5th Century Chinese hermit/poet.

"All this brings back such joy I forget
glittering careers. White clouds drift
endless skies. I watch".
I watch.

Give or take a few years, the Christian ascetics were meditating in the African deserts around the same time that most well-known Chinese hermit poets were wandering the Chinese mountains and valleys, tending their small huts and gardens. When I asked Red Pine about the desert having a presence, he told me about his own time wandering in southern Utah canyons. "There's a presence but so few people taking the time it takes to experience it."

If getting to God required getting rid of everything else, then the God of those early Christian hermits must have been somewhere inside of them. When I'm alone with nothing around, what then, is that hum?

During my quest to understand Hermits, I've encountered many new terms. *Qi* is the circulating life force whose existence and properties are the basis of much Chinese philosophy and medicine. *Unus Mundus*, Latin for "one world," is the concept of an underlying unified reality from which everything emerges and to which everything returns. *Lumen naturae* refers to the spark of life. Add to these *Gnosticism* (the feminine-toned archaic wisdom) and that measurable force, the Shumann Resonance entering through the yuan channy near the balls of our feet. That there is a hum, always a hum, begins making sense. We blend with these outer forces.

Enter, *Mountain Home: The Wilderness Poetry of Ancient China*, translated by David Hinton. After seeing this book on our shelf for years, I picked it up last spring, during the early days of the Hermit Virus. In his introduction, Hinton introduces a term I'd never heard before: *tzu-jan* or "self-ablaze." *Tzu-jan* is the "ten thousand things emerging spontaneously from the generative source, each according to its own nature, independent and self-sufficient, each dying and returning into the process of change, only to reappear in another self-generating form."

"I'm completely out of my league" was my first thought reading this. It may as well have been in a foreign language. After reading the description again, *Tzu jan* began to feel familiar.[22] It felt like "wildness" to me. Here in the west, *tzu-jan* is translated as 'nature' or 'freedom,' or 'spontenaity,' which in the same way as our limited view of wilderness does, "reduces this to a kind of sweet pastoral poem of romantic escapism."

Bill Porter (aka Red Pine) and David Hinton define 'hermit' differently. For Red Pine, a hermit is someone "who prefers the wilderness to civilization." To Hinton, a hermit has sacrificed, given something up. The Chinese poets Hinton writes so eloquently about, suffered no 'abnegation,' that being in the wilderness was the best place to be. He referred to them not as hermits but as "recluses."

As if we've agreed to a time, the day and I get up together. I dress quickly in the cold and wander off—to loosen my night-thickened body and to gather more of that downed pinion for the fire I've decided to rebuild.

Back at 'camp,' I break the wood I gathered into small pieces and pile the smallest twigs in the center of the fire, which is too cool to re-ignite. I fall back in my chair and pour water in the pot, light my stove, then the fire.

I'm excited about breakfast. An envelope of instant cranberry and cinnamon oatmeal with a cut-up hard-boiled up mixed in. And good coffee.

My fire grows slowly as I add twigs and then larger branches. I pour steaming water on my oatmeal concoction and sit back.

My privilege makes this possible. We have choices. Many have no choice.

Louis, our 'son' from Rwanda, manages an Amazon warehouse near Washington D.C. He does his best to avoid COVID while overseeing a group of workers, most of them People Of Color, who make sure we privileged have all we need or want, adding billions of pandemic dollars to the net worth of his boss, Jeff Bezos.

I scrape the last of my oatmeal/egg breakfast from the plastic measuring cup I use as a bowl with my spoon, which I then lick clean. I heat up the water left in the pot and swirl it around in my cup. Not wanting to waste water, I stir in my instant coffee. I breathe in the steam rising from the surface and then sip, filtering the few floating oats with my lip.

I feel my privilege, here in my camp chair, surrounded by cliffs and wildness, my cookstove, food, and fire all within reach. A familiar lump rises in my throat. The lump of guilt I cannot swallow.

With COVID numbers rising again, we'd been advised (warned?) to stay home. Early on, this isolation had felt more like serving a sentence for a crime. Lately, thoughts of our isolation have carried with them, hints of panic about returning to our old life. Terry and I have talked about never returning to the 'race' we've been running. The teaching, the writing, the selling of books—the travel required. How much of it can now be done from the green chair in the zoom room in the corner of our house. Again, the privilege and the guilt, knowing how many risk their health and lives to guarantee us that opportunity.

Although I've ignored my fire, the coals throb and glow. I add a handful of perfect sticks, which ignite with that hollow *pffffft* sound. "That first fire." I think back a million years to that very first fire and the magic it brought to those early lives. Where did they think it came from? Even in this modern, *disenchanted* world, fire continually astounds.

"Enchantment," as a historic concept, marks a key period in our evolution. *Disenchantment* is associated with 'modernity and the Enlightenment, which many believe marked our 'rise' above all other life and our own 'pre-civilized' history.

If 'enchantment' is related to our 'pre-civilized' history, then 'disenchantment' is aligned with the beginning of agriculture and civilization. Agriculture led to the commodification of nature— the tree spirits disappeared when the trees they inhabited were cut into boards. This transition occurred ten to twelve thousand years ago—a flash in time compared to the previous *two hundred thousand years* we lived in an enchanted world. *'Enchantment' surely played a role in our success as a species.*

Modernity—disenchantment—is marked by the splitting of our lives from one integrated existence into two: *outer* and *inner; conscious* and *unconscious; ordinary* and *non-ordinary* reality; and *enchanted* and *disenchanted.* Although as a species, we'd lived well with one complete life for ten thousand generations, we became more powerful and all-controlling once we separated off anything we could not see, explain, measure, and *sell.*

This is too simple. Perhaps no division actually exists, but our white Euro-American privilege is only possible by separating the world into a nearly infinite list of either/or, us/them, white/black, up/down, in/out, etc. In reality, there is no division, only belief in division.

Outer world. Inner world.

The book, "Powers of Ten," comes back to me again. I'd forgotten. The photos taken from decreasing distance, beginning at the far edge of the known universe, did not end with the vision of the couple picnicking in a park. They continued to her hand, and then inside her hand skin and further and further into some vast sub-cellular place. The miracle is that the photos of the innermost quarks and sub-atomic particles in their own invisible orbits closely resembled those taken of stars at the far edge of the universe.

Voices of hikers rise up from far below. I move to my edge and look out, hoping to remain hidden, pretending they are Proud Boys out to find me as part of Trump's effort to round up dissidents. With my binoculars, I see a small group, not Proud Boys but a family, I suspect—two teen-aged girls, an older boy, and their father? They move easily and happily and seem focused more on their conversation than their surroundings. The joy emanating from them makes me forget how I'd blanched at the disruption of my solitude. They are white and privileged like me.

Rue Mapp ("Outdoor Afro") and James Mills (Joy Trip Project) are two friends who are black, who've dedicated their lives to expose more People of Color to the natural world. I still shudder whenever I think about Chris Cooper's experience with the white woman while he was "birdwatching while black" in Central Park. How much less complicated wildness has been for me than for them. How everything has been less complicated for me than it has for them, for anyone of any other race than white.

Recently the word 'white' when attached to race, lost part of its meaning for me. Now whenever I read or hear or witness racism, I think of in evolutionary time how recently humans separated into race. And yet, what a huge and explosive issue race has become. While I still acknowledge being *white*, one white man who is part of the 'white' race, which controls the world, "colorless" might be a more accurate term for our skin. In

1906, the bones of Cheddar Man,[23] a Pleistocene hunter, were discovered in a cave in England. A decade ago, I read that analysis of Cheddar Man's mitochondrial DNA determined that he has a direct descendent, a schoolteacher currently living in the same area. Learning about Cheddar Man was important to me, as he blows wide open my concept of "family"—we all have ancestors living long before those people whose names we know. Cheddar Man embodies our direct connection to evolutionary ancestors. Then three years ago, I heard the familiar words "Cheddar Man" during a BBC report on the radio. The story was about how using new, sophisticated tests on his old bones, scientists discovered that Cheddar Man was black. While reading everything I could find on Cheddar Man and his race, I asked a question I'd never thought to ask: "what makes us white?" There are many theories, the main one being that we were black when we first left Africa, 40,000 years ago, and began spreading across the planet. Some of us, Cheddar Man, moved north into England, hunting and gathering. Some stopped in the Middle East 12,000 years ago, a place called the Fertile Crescent. There, they began growing their food, and formed the first agricultural communities. Those early cultivated crops, it turns out, did not provide the same nutrition as our evolutionary diet of hunting and gathering. Six thousand years ago, farmers from the Fertile Crescent began spreading out, many moving north into what is now Europe. Their poor agricultural diet and the weaker northern sun resulted in serious Vitamin D deficiency. Within a few generations, we became lighter, increasing the photosynthesis of Vitamin D in our skin, compensating for the weaker northern sun. To compensate for the sun, we lost our color. We did not turn white.

"White" supremacy seems rooted in weakness rather than strength.

This story fits into a longer one. In agricultural communities, one provided food for many, leaving many the time for other creative pursuits. *Many* made art, built permanent structures, invented—*Many* invented weapons. Weapons compensated for weakness and enabled our ancestors to suppress others. Weapons made slavery possible. To settle the Americas, colorless people required "guns, germs, and steel" to overcome *other*, the colorful, indigenous people who had occupied these lands since the beginning of human time. This simple story makes sense to me. It is the truest story I've found.

As if I've been holding onto my thoughts with a leash, I relax, and off they go. Besides weapons, did we make the crates in that cartoon,[24] the one with kids trying to watch a baseball game from the other side of a fence? The cartoon illustrates the difference between 'equality' and 'equity.'

Three people of different heights are trying to see over a fence to watch a ball game. One is tall, one mid-sized, and one short. They're all standing on two crates. The tall one can easily see over the fence. The middle one can glance over the fence. The short one can't see over the fence at all. This is "equality"—each person, regardless of his height, has two crates. "Equity" is different. Equity is the tall guy giving one of his crates, which he doesn't need, to the short guy who, with three crates to stand on, can now see over the fence.

What happened in the beginning? Is the goal to create equity or reestablish it. If all humans share the same evolutionary roots, then 'equity' must be an element in our common evolutionary experience. Along the way, while compensating for the weakness our colorlessness represents, while using our weapons to suppress others, we acquired most of the crates. In doing so, we took control of the experience of others, including looking out over the fence, at the game, *at the power*. Among some, consciousness grew, and along with it, the realization that moving forward required 'equality' and passed out crates from their own supply, one per person—a good first step. And then and then and then, the long-term damage done to those denied crates for so long became obvious. Part of us knew that the next step would require giving up more crates to those denied crates for so long, reestablishing 'equity.' This offended some crate owners, who forgot that they did not earn their crates but got them from their parents and grandparents. They used only those crates needed to stare out at all the power. Giving crates to those so long denied crates offended these people, so they hoarded their crates, knowing they'd likely never need them, other than to pass them onto to their children. These people looked for ways to take the crates recently given to those who'd been denied crates for so long. The world became divided between those whose worth was determined by the size of their crate collection and those with the minimum number of crates. How does the story of this cartoon end? Will those denied crates tear the fence down, rending all crates worthless? Those in love with their crates continue gathering them even though the crates have lost all meaning. Everyone else lives happily ever after.

Out backpacking, we're aligned more with the life for which evolution designed us as at any other time in our modern lives. If extreme privilege is required to live in comfort out in the wilds even for two days or a week, we cannot expect to understand, let alone *use* our evolutionary bodies in the way that we've always used them: *to save ourselves. To thrive.*

Perhaps days in the wild, miles wandered, birds identified, wild tracks and comets seen, are all like those crates, have all be available to people of privilege. And like the crates in the cartoon, I must convert my experience into the currency of equity.

The last three large branches I placed on the fire seem unchanged, except that the flames have turned them into dark ghosts of themselves. I add another branch on top of them, and they disintegrate into tiny coals and ash. Whatever it is that keeps the wood solid and intact burns away, providing heat and light and smoke.

Warm in my chair, sipping coffee and tending my small fire, watching nearly black clouds accumulate in the corners of a dull grey sky, I feel my plans shifting. I have little desire to get up and spend the day exploring. I sit for a few minutes thinking of reasons I can't sit here indefinitely. There aren't any.

I place the end of the largest branch in the center of my fire, knowing that I will sit long enough to watch it turn elegantly to ash. I have a new plan: I'll sit feeding my fire until my wood is gone, at which time, I'll make a new plan.

While one end of a juniper branch glows in the flame, smoke finds its way along invisible interior corridors and pools in small exposed voids at the other end. Then it rises and floats off. I think of that scene in the film *Smoke*. William Hurt's character is in the smoke shop explaining how to calculate the weight of smoke: you weigh an unsmoked cigar. Then you smoke it and subtract from its weight unsmoked, the weight of the ash and the blunt. The difference is the weight of the smoke. "Like weighing spirit," he says. Those three branches I'd burned earlier maintained their exact shape only to disintegrate into powdery ash when touched. Had I weighed them before burning and subtracted the weight of the coals and ash left once they burned, I would have had the weight of whatever the substance that held that wood together. Its *spirit?* Besides all the mystery and meaning attached to it, *spirit* may be what holds everything together.

Something large, white, and cottony floats down through the corner of my vision. I turn to wonder what it is, thinking first, "down feather". Passing directly in front of me it seems too big for a feather, even that of an owl or eagle. It lands ten meters away, beyond my sleeping bag, which is still spread out on the sand. I get up as quickly as I can, which after sitting so long is not quick at all, and hurry over to the last seen point of this white mystery. Either I miscalculated its location or it had disintegrated on landing—or *mysteriously disappeared*, but I cannot find it.

If smoke and spirit are related and burning releases smoke/spirit, what are we to make of the burning of fossil fuels? Decomposed ancient organisms compressed beneath the pressure of two hundred million years into what we know as carbon. Nineteenth-century technology harnessed the power from burning carbon to make metal on a scale that changed the world. Twentieth-century technology harnessed the power from combusting oil to move automobiles, which changed the world again. The unintended consequence, as we now know, is the 'smoke,' the polluting result of burning carbon that today is causing the warming of the planet which is changing and challenging all life in devastating ways, quickly enough to watch in real-time. Smoke, pollution. Spirit?

"Earth to Brooke!" A raven voice like a rusty hinge rescues me from that rabbit hole where I might have drowned.

Will I live long enough to hear some of the Republicans I know to thank us for pushing pushing pushing pushing on endangered species and wildness, for forcing the dark possibilities of a climate impacted future into our collective reality. Will they thank us for clean water and clean air? Will they ever admit that "the market" in which they placed all their hope and bet all of our lives failed? I would love one day to hear from them that racism, kids in cages, climate change are not *differences of opinions but* are failures of imagination and morality. There is no reaching across the divide separating us. That would suggest that I, too, had the capacity to accept the horrors that they have. That I would be willing to sacrifice moral character, hoping it will get me what I believe I deserve but did not earn.

Lately, I've looked across "the divide separating us" and automatically assumed that those on that far side are defective in any number of ways. Sometimes I catch myself because of close family members who dwell there, on that other side. They own guns, listen to Fox News, believe that liberals are "godless," are good Mormons. They've focused on money and are very concerned by the taxes they pay and that their taxes are spent on those less deserving.

Hank, Terry's brother, falls into his own category. Quite the hermit himself, Hank spends his days working in the ditch for the family pipeline construction company. He's well-read, and spends his free time wandering the desert with his dogs and guns. Hank got COVID early in the Pandemic, so early that we weren't sure exactly what it was that leveled him. Once free of his symptoms, he came to stay with us. We spent a lot of time together while he recovered, talking and walking. He got stronger. "Trump will win," he told me. "There're so many out there, like me, working in the trenches, people who have been ignored for too long," he said. "Trump sees us," Hank said. I'm not sure who Hank actually voted for. Regardless, he is responsible for exploding the stereotypes I use to help justify my own position.

The rising sun finds a weakness in the cloud-thickened sky. A beam focused through this seam hits me in the side of my head. Directly in front of me, a boulder the size of a small truck lights up. I can't recall this boulder from my earlier trip, although had it not been in the path of that sun shot, I may have missed it now. How has it hung perched at such a precarious, nearly vertical angle on that tilted surface? For how long?

The light moves on to illuminate something else.

The fire twisting in the shifting breezes, clouds folding and spreading high above, and in between, the rattle of dried leaves that froze before falling from a dozen nearby single-leaf ash— wind at every level. Everything moves around me, pushes past me in all directions. My camp chair is now the driver's seat in a magic ship hurtling through space.

"Enchantment." The word suggests excitement, the extraordinary. As I hold onto the arms of my chair while careening through time and space, the world is unquestionably enchanted, is purely extraordinary and exciting. My only experience with the word "enchanted" before being exposed to it as describing an entire epoch of human existence was the song, *Some Enchanted Evening*. Before modernity marked the world's "disenchantment," life was constantly enchanted. Enchantment was not extraordinary. It was ordinary. An 'enchanted' life only seems unique and special in contrast with the disenchantment modernity forces on us, requires to keep the system spinning along, toward what seems more and more like a tragic end. That we refer to our pre-civilized and therefore evolutionary lives as "enchanted" suggests just how far from 'evolution' we've strayed. As if this force which is the source for life as we know it, has somehow become obsolete in the shadow of our great and powerful and devastating intelligence.

Religious hermits are often referred to as "Anchorites," which means 'religious recluse.' With the root word, "anchor,"

I realized sitting there, that "anchorite" might suggest that hermits don't move around much. In fact, the longer I sit here in my chair, the more difficult I find getting up. I'm definitely anchored.

I don't feel presumptuous calling myself a hermit. A 'reluctant hermit' is more accurate. Red Pine told me in a recent note that there are both 'little hermits' and 'great' hermits. Little hermits need wild solitude, while great hermits are hermits wherever they are, even in the city. If I am a hermit, I am most certainly a 'little hermit.' Aspiring, however. If the Hindus are correct that we all eventually mature into hermits, I'm in process.

By David Hinton's definition, I might be more of a recluse since I did not sacrifice when choosing to live near all this wildness. Before the pandemic, that is. The Hermit Virus has forced us to 'give up' much, to 'sacrifice' in a way, the life we'd been living. I'm doing my part to contain the virus. This, then, makes me a hermit (a 'little' hermit).

Inside the back cover of my notebook, I've taped a miniature copy of my favorite Hermit Tarot Card—Number 9. Terry is very good at reading the cards. She found a Tarot deck under her Grandmother Mimi's bed, after she died. Based on notes Mimi made in her books, her interest in the Tarot started with Jung's belief that the Tarot worked on the principle of synchronicity. I like my hermit card because if I squint, the background looks like sandstone mesas in Southern Utah. My hermit seems very wise and looks off toward something over my right shoulder so intently that I turn to look there, too. As is tradition, my hermit carries a lamp in one hand, a staff in the other. The 'Hermit Card' is a call to introversion, knowing that the most powerful role humans can play in the collective good is through self-knowledge and that self-knowledge requires solitude. The Hermit Card represents wisdom.

"Wisdom"—that tricky word, again.

I define *wisdom* as deep evolutionary knowledge that contributes to the greater survival of the species. It comes directly from the Earth. It has collective as opposed to personal or corporate value. 'Wisdom' never has a qualifier attached: no "good" wisdom, or "big" or "small" wisdom. Only "wisdom" as if it's something one does or does not have. Walt Whitman said, "Wisdom is of the soul, is not susceptible of proof, is its own proof[25]...." . As opposed to 'consciousness' which, beyond the simple concept of a living organism being aware of itself, has layers, "higher/lower," etc. This idea comes floating into my mind on a firm breeze I can't ignore.

The need I once had to put people into categories according to how highly evolved consciously they are was in itself a sign of low consciousness. In Buddhism[26], "wisdom" is strong when "distinction making" is weak. Wisdom is not a function of knowledge or thinking, and in fact, is the antithesis of thought and the mind. If pure wisdom requires no mind— no-self—which is both the result and requirement of 'awe,' then 'wisdom' and 'awe' must be linked. I don't know much about Transcendental Mediation, but a good friend has been practicing it for decades for access to what he calls "pure consciousness." Wisdom. Pure consciousness. Awe. All of these are impossible in the presence of thought powered by the mind, products of the expanded self.

My "categorization"—my thinking, my need to under-stand—represents my lack of wisdom. So be it. But If I wonder about possible levels of consciousness but stop, not wanting to seem less wise, that would be disingenuous. Had I been wise enough, I would not have wondered about the 'levels of con-sciousness' in the first place.

I am not alone in my need to categorize. Richard Barrett, the writer and business consultant, describes[27] seven levels of consciousness.[28] The "survival" mode is the lowest level of consciousness. 'Contribution', or the desire to serve the greater good with a long-term perspective, is the highest. These levels seem to evolve from purely individual—if one is starving or broke, focusing outside of one's self is difficult—to the purely *self-less* collective.

While thinking in terms of 'levels" or 'layers' of conscious-ness suggests I have much personal work to do, I revisited Barrett hoping to better understand the radical right who will continue their role in America regardless of who is pres-ident. Of the seven levels, members of this segment of our political spectrum seem to occupy the bottom three "Levels of Consciousness"—"Survival," "Relationship," and "Self-Esteem." These levels are self-oriented, individual, and based on defi-ciency and fear. This compared to the more collective focus of the next four levels. "Transformation," the Fourth Level, is feel-ing free from the fear keeping us from being who we actually are independent of family and culture or group we've joined simply to 'belong.' "Transformation" prepares us for 'Self-Expression' as we discover our 'calling' toward a life driven by higher values. "Collaboration" is the need to connect with others sharing the same values, knowing that our effect will multiply. The highest *Seventh Level of Consciousness* is "Contribution," where we tap into the depth of our wisdom while disappearing inside love and kindness and discover our unique way to serve the world.

Barrett's levels sit on a firm foundation made of other philosophies, including Jung's concept of "Individuation".

Individuation is the bringing up unconscious material into consciousness. If that deep unconscious does hold our evolutionary history, including all we've ever needed to save ourselves, then, *rising consciousness is necessary for our survival as a species.* Rising consciousness—Evolution of consciousness. Climate change, seen through the lens of deep time, is a recent problem caused by our modern, recent lives. It is as serious as any we've faced throughout our entire history. It is advancing at a desperate speed, outpacing our ability to adapt biologically. My great hope for us, for this planet, is that we are hard-wired to "evolve" –to *adapt to changing conditions,* but that "evolution" is not limited to *biological evolution.* Conscious evolution is another option. Perhaps it is the only option.

"Awe" is the source of "wisdom." "Awe" shrinks the self, opening the pathway to the collective unconscious. 'Wisdom' must be the bringing of evolutionary materials to the surface where they help us survive, **evolve.**

The Evolution of consciousness is the growth of wisdom. Wisdom is evolution.

I'm torn in two directions, split down the middle. Over there, swirling like leaves are all the concepts I've placed around me to grasp as I float out alone through my life: *hermits, self-knowledge, the sacred, spirituality, collective unconscious, awe, disappearance, evolution of consciousness, wisdom*—my comfort growing in proportion to the sense I'm able to make, the connections.

But then, out there the other way, my young knowledge tells me I'm integral to something very real, *tzu-jan* with its 10,000 perpetually generating things. But while all my wondering, all my intensity to 'make sense', provides a rackety platform of comfort, it separates me, *dis-integrates* me, makes me a separate one looking out at the other 9,999 things.

I am flowing on in the warm dark river rushing onward with it all. But then I grab a limb poking out from the riverbank and pull myself out of the river. Standing up on the bank, I look down at the river passing beneath me and take notes, trying to make sense as it moves on beneath me, without me.

Who will believe me if I don't explain it to them? *Not the moon. The finger pointing at the moon.*

In his book, *Existence: A Story* David Hinton writes that there is no separation, that we're all part of the same "Existence tissue". This separation, this needing to know, name things, explain, to 'depict' sets us at odds with nature and the universe. Rather, art and poetry in their purest form, 'enacts'. Hinton writes that Native American rock art does not *depict* but *enacts*—a distinction I'm beginning to understand.

Years ago, on my first visit to the "Great Gallery", a spectacular well-known rock art site 100 miles west of here, as the raven flies. Terry and I were there alone, sitting in front of the "Holy Ghost' the human-sized figure standing in contrast to the other, smaller dark figures to the sides of it. Like most who visit this place, I was wondering what the figures meant (what they depicted), what the ancient artists were attempting to communicate, when something shifted. I watched as two-dimensions became three—the dark figures were no longer alongside the "Holy Ghost" but formed a circle around it. Then the circle of figures began moving around the Holy Ghost. There was no meaning or message—no thinking, only movement and grace. Time stopped during that ghost dance, and I had disappeared into the awe of it all, this enactment.

The self shrinks when we experience awe, sometimes all the way to nothing, to disappearance. This is clear. What is not so clear is if experiencing awe requires a small, humble self. This may depend on the magnitude of the moment. Terry and I were in Yellowstone, in the Lamar Valley, waiting, watching dusk drape the land and the carcass of a female bison which two days before had been killed by wolves. A small group of bison moved toward her in a straight line, circled her three times, then pawed her and bowed. We couldn't speak or breathe. A man, a hunter, wearing fatigues hopped from the truck parked next to us, desperate to connect. "Did you see what I just saw?" he asked. "They were paying respect". For me, this moment of awe, was proof that everything was right with the world and would be, regardless. I sensed that this man, this hunter, may have "disappeared" for the first time.

I need to stretch. Wandering along horizontal ledges and down safe creases in the purple sandstone, I stand on the flat bottom of the gorge. I'll follow it to its end, and marvel at the strange formations eons of flowing water have carved into the walls. There, in three dimensions, the face that inspired the screamer in Munch's painting, *The Scream* protrudes from the wall. I climb the sandy slope to a partial cave in the layer above me, its vertical wall forming the cliff protecting my camp. I'll sit here awhile.

In *The Wisdom of the Desert*, Merton writes about *quies*, a kind of 'rest' those early Hermits sought which was different from any 'rest' I'm familiar with. This is the 'rest' made possible by what Merton called "a no-whereness—no mindedness that has lost all pre-occupation with a limited self". The kind of rest that comes with disappearance. Merton compares these early anchorites to the Zen monks.

A few dots need connecting so I'll sit a bit longer. Yes, there's "awe" in its overwhelming form, which is not sought but cannot be ignored. Then there's the "awe" for which we can prepare by opening our mind and making room by shrinking our selves, the "awe" which might be provoked. For the hermits Merton wrote about, this 'rest' is possible only by disappearing, by "no-hereness and no mindedness". The shrinking self provokes 'awe', what about the disappearing self? Is the 'aweness' of 'awe' inversely proportional to the size of the self? Then "No-self"— the self shrunk to nothing—must mean perpetual awe.

Big self/small self/no self. Whew.
No self, then no "duality".

Seng Tsan, 6th Century, Chinese Buddhist Monk, wrote[29]

Don't cling to dualities
And don't seek them out
Once a yes or no appears
Confusion clouds the mind.

Hermits are sought out for their wisdom, which results from their rest, their "quies", their disappearance, and their perpetual state of 'awe.' "Wisdom fostered by awe".

The breeze turns to wind, the temperature drops, and I pull my jacket around me. The future is written above and all around me: a storm is near. Do I leave later this afternoon, or spend a wet night out followed by a muddy slog home tomorrow?

Having nothing to prove, I opt to wander around a bit more. Then I'll sit by my fire a while then pack and walk home by dark.

I wander along the cliff base as it curves above my camp. Rather than following a gradual ridge that leads directly to camp, I drop into the unexplored wash leading west, longer but more interesting. Passing beneath the massive precariously perched boulder I've seen from camp, I notice on the opposite side of the wash two smaller boulders, much lighter in color, in vivid contrast to the purplish formation on which they sit. They perch on small invisible platforms, suspending most of their mass inches above the solid foundation surrounding them. I've seen this phenomenon before in other places and this must be what happened: *At some point, long ago, these boulders fell from high above when the softer layer beneath them eroded away. Based* on their light color and hardness these are formed of Entrada or Navajo Sandstone. They tumbled down the slopes, coming to rest on the softer purple and more horizontal Organ Pipe formation. Years passed and the Entrada boulders protected the softer Organ Pipe surface on which they sat, from the wind and water flowing around them. Gradually, water and wind and time eroded around the boulders and then beneath them, leaving them perilously perched on small platforms growing smaller with each storm.

Coming back in a year or two or four I may find that these boulders have tumbled into the wash bottom when their weight became too great for their shrinking platforms.

The platform erodes.

Scott Abbott writes, "maybe Spinoza's 'deus sive natura' — god or nature — has finally got fed up and decided to interfere with the Senate Judiciary Committee and inhabitants of the White House." With further inquiry I discovered that Spinoza meant God was Natura Naturans, not Natura naturata— "a dynamic nature in action, growing and changing, not a passive or static thing."

There is something out here, something very real that lives and moves and balances, that does not favor humans above other life—"God, a dynamic nature in action growing and changing".

Have we gone too far? Have we moderns accomplished too much to ever go back to the mysteries, to accepting that there are forces out there over which we have no control, that we have no capacity to understand, let alone, quantify?

I move effortlessly over the hard and flat wash bottom in an invisible current. The recent flood which jammed this nest of twigs waist high into this wall crevasse cleansed and smoothed this canyon. I can feel the flow, the velocity. I can hear the sound.

Rarely am I conscious of being so firmly in 'place'. Yes, being aware of 'being in place' indicates being slightly *out of place*. So be it. With the many competing motivations modern life requires, moments like this remind me that I'm exactly where I need to be.

Our greatest role. True self –self knowledge—must be related to occupation—that the depth to which we know ourselves is proportional to knowing how the planet might make the best use of us. I'm haunted by the question "if everyone focused only on self-knowledge and their universal role, who would do the work of keeping the machine of civilization going?" All the layers of society have come into view during this pandemic. The growers grow. The bakers bake. Packages packed and moved, brought. *True self* –"that's all well and good but how are you going to make a living?" and, "do this and you'll be fine", and "Oh by the way, here is some bread. Here are the circuses.[30]" This is the conundrum we created when we abandoned our evolutionary lives.

The magic in the world, the *enchantment*, existed until our ancestors commodified it. Magic was confusing and *pesky* and got in the way of progress. Power was required to control it.

Power came from the profits gained by accumulating and selling what one did not personally need. My family 'sold'. Generations of my family were middle class but also 'middle-men' who did not actually create, design, develop, or make anything. My grandfather once told me that nothing happens until someone sells something. That this was to be my life was assumed from the day I was born. As a result, I lived 'halflives'[31] for fifteen years: one half selling building supplies, the other half pursuing wildness and self-knowledge. I struggled. Looking back, I suffered by not fully responding to the allele that some of us have always had, that makes us want to explore and be rewarded. Although it will not admit it, society still needs some of us out there looking for what's next, who know that our greatest role is working toward a future where all life thrives and that being part of the Earth's biota does not diminish but elevates us.

I've wandered this twisting canyon bottom maze for an hour. I'm no longer confident where my camp is, on the next layer above me. If I could fly I could be back in my chair in seconds, but I've not completed my reconnaissance, a responsibility I take seriously. Wandering is my evolutionary duty.

Those religious ascetics wandering the desert—escaping— through 'morphic resonance' may have made a difference in the world simply by being out there, alone.[32] "Morphic Resonance" is, as described by Amit Goswami, "non-locality—action at a distance", "action transmitted without signals that propagate through space".[33] With a high degree of spiritual development these hermits could affect the collective. This suggests that we can change the world by changing ourselves. Whatever it is in the quantum world that allows this to happen, is beyond me. Something important happens out in the wilds—I know this. If those early hermits had a positive impact on the world simply by being out in the wild solitude, why can't I?

I love how the closer the shadow is to its source, the more vivid it is.

How did I know back in 2016 that I needed to wander off into the wilds? Was I looking for peace from the chaos and negativity generated by the election? Did I need clarity and perspective—an answer to the question: "What is the actual significance of this next four years in the context of deep time?" Or did I actually expect answers to the question of "How are we to deal with Trump as president?" All I remember is that I was desperate to escape.

Throughout my history, I've been obsessed with skiing, running, wandering, being outside. I've been good at finding the slightest seams in time, the most subtle of reasons—any excuse to feed my obsession. Any planning I did was through the filter of "where will I run? How much free time will I have?" My obsession is related to the inability I've always had to do meaningless work even if it meant financial reward. I've spent much of my work life floating among my projects, not wanting to land for long, because something bigger and more important, more authentic, visceral, had lodged back of my mind and filling up my entire body: Wildness.

Years ago, I met my friend, Mark, to camp and hike. He brought his friend, a psychiatrist, whom I liked very much. Around the fire one night I mentioned my book, Halflives and its subject. A few weeks later the psychiatrist sent a note: "I read your book. I have some pills that would fix your problem." I sensed he was joking, knowing that my "problem" was my inability and lack of desire to be motivated by money, or to focus on modern world responsibilities. Perhaps pharmaceutical companies had discovered how to profit by delivering the Spore in pill form.

That a pill could 'fix' my problem suggested that I had something that could be named. Society thinks that my love for wildness at the expense of 'success' needs 'fixing'.

This Wilderness walk-about is different. The thinnest possible veneer of a reason is yes, I wanted to use it as a lens for assessing what had happened to me personally during the past four years. This is a good enough excuse to get out, but I don't really need excuses.

My small canyon branches. The left fork leads more directly to camp. I take the right fork. The view above me is the giant Wingate wall in whose shadow I've been living since coming down from the pass yesterday. The wash bottom becomes steeper as it cuts through the layers forming the cliff base, before it ends vertically, abruptly in a pour-over. I take the obvious route around it to the left—steep, but with step-like ledges which I climb quickly. On top, I climb the sandy slope to a minor ridge which I follow to the base of the Wingate cliff. Here, weather has carved a small alcove. I'll sit for a while.

All around me the air is still, not a breeze disturbs it. Yet in front of me, between me and the far cliff that is the opposite side of this valley, a sharp wind shreds a cloud into long giant forms, kites, broken free from their strings. The wind stops. The cloud reforms and as if at the mercy of a massive force, presses into everything, is perpetually generating, is tzu-jan. I am watching this, but more. I am integral to this, but more. I am this. "Not connection," David Hinton says, "but identity."

Back in my chair, I hear the voices of climbers the wind brings from faraway towers, each in their own cloud. Rare sun bursts through and turns a raven's black back silver as it banks in flight. The wind seems to battle the cliffs when in fact it is sculpting them.

We've always talked about "wilderness for its own sake", its 'intrinsic' values—regardless of what it means to modern humans. Intrinsic values are difficult to use while debating wilderness because, unlike coal and timber, oil and gas, they cannot be priced. We've adopted the economic argument by considering wilderness not as an end in itself, but as a means—a nice backpacking trail, a wild river to kayak, a vertical rock cliff to climb—all using the latest gear. The drama of kite-like clouds or ravens banking in the wind are intrinsic values because they are 'ends' in and of themselves. Or are they 'means', because of how they enhance my life?

Could this be the real reason we care about wildness? Because in these times of the deadening and hijacking of our consciousness, wildness engages us perceptively. The next step may be realizing that this same pure perception is always possible. That this perception is being part of everything spontaneously emerging from the generative source, then dying, then returning to the process of change, only to reappear in another self-generating form. Wildness is the end in itself, its value intrinsic. Tzu-jan.

That 'hum' I hear is the sound of ten thousand things perpetually generating.

I fire up my stove and pull out tea from my food bag. Rooibos, from the Hell's Backbone Grill store. Before the Hermit Virus, my interest in food began to transcend survival, occasionally becoming a creative expression. Throughout the pandemic, cooking has been a creative part of my day. Each afternoon, Terry and I talk about dinner and the possibilities based on what ingredients we have on hand. Blake Spaulding and Jen Castle get partial blame for this. They own the Hell's Backbone Grill in the tiny town of Boulder, Utah, on the edge of The Grand Staircase/ Escalante National Monument. I'm proud to call them friends. Besides tea we keep on hand their spices, pancake mix, sweet corn and mustard. We use their cookbooks.

Blake and Jen and their restaurant were featured in The New Yorker after joining a lawsuit against Trump[34] saying that their business was radically and negatively affected by the reduction of Grand Staircase/Escalante National Monument. Their restaurant has won numerous awards, including being a finalist for the prestigious James Beard Award. The Hell's Backbone Grill is the largest employer in town. I've known Blake and Jen since they opened in 2000, four years after Clinton signed that monument into law. They're Buddhists. They have their own gardens producing 10,000 pounds of vegetables, annually. They raise their own meat or source it from local ranchers. They're committed to environmental ethics and not shy about speaking out because threats to the area's wild character threatens both the future and their business. They've become the town center. Once the end of a lonely rural road, Boulder is now a destination due to Blake and Jen and the Hells Backbone Grill. For me, they represent the 'sacred feminine'.

I'm a messy cook but I'm working on it. I don't have any specialty. In fact, I make something new nearly every time I cook, not wanting to be bored by it. I look forward to night and cooking something new. Gauging by edibility, I score pretty well. We have a Sun Oven, which came from a good friend of ours who's involved in this global project to help rural people in developing countries cook without wood, which is more and more difficult to find these days. Our harsh, hot summer had at least one positive aspect: I cooked a whole chicken in the sun oven in two hours, a chocolate cake—which tasted a lot better than it looked—great cod, and salmon.

"Send friends Christmas gifts from the Hells Backbone store," I write in my notebook.

Either I've come a long ways in four years, or like an aging knife, am losing my edge. Sitting here in complete comfort, I feel certain that I've gotten exactly what I'd needed from both hikes. The difference? The first hike began with a goal and a line on a map. This second one, began with me knowing that something good would happen. I'm comfortable not being conscious of exactly what it is I need.

I'll be back home in a few hours and life will seem normal and I might know who the next president will be. The surface of life will look as it would have had I not gone off in the wilds to stare into that small fire and up through the clouds at all those stars. Beneath the surface, much will have changed, and changed in undefinable ways I'm getting better at trusting.

I feel differently about Terry's shadow. I was wrong thinking I needed to step out of her shadow. During the past year, I've found comfort in her shadow—the dappled light, the moist air. The mushrooms growing there. In the years since writing that, I've acknowledged that like nature where some organisms thrive in light and others in shade or shadow, aspiring to share the light with Terry would inhibit me, like the bat hunting at noon. It would also inhibit her.

If I believe that self-knowledge is also knowing how the planet might make the best use of us, then although it feels strange, I'm getting more comfortable working beneath the surface, just inside the light. It has not been easy. Why would it be easy? For 10,000 years we men have been programmed to be in control—*10,000 years of patriarchy.* The 'crate' cartoon...the one with the kids of different heights stand on crates hoping to watch a game over the fence. This might also apply to women. At birth, my white American penis was given three crates, which when I stood on them gave me access to the power and the resources on the other side of the fence. Terry, a girl born into a privileged family had one crate to stand on. Although down below me, she was close enough to hear what I told her I was seeing as I looked over the fence. Plus, as a female, she didn't need to know *everything* that was going on over there. That changed when some men began seeing women as intelligent powerful beings. We gave them one of our crates so now we were 'equal'. Even though we men could still easily see over the fence, women, less tall, could see over the fence only by pulling themselves up and holding on, the amount of time they can see over the fence depended on their personal stamina and strength. Some had great stamina and strength. This "equality" was a step in the right direction. Rather than depending on men for their crates, many women have now gone out and at great personal expense and significant investment of time, found their own crates. Some men, standing on their own crates, got angry seeing that women had more crates and could see over the fence, and have gone so far as to try and damage or steal a woman's crates. I believe in the role of the 'sacred feminine' in creating a livable future. I will give Terry all my crates, to free up the strength and time she needs to expend seeing over the wall, which she will use for much better and more important tasks. She can have all my crates. I don't need to see over the wall anymore. We men have not done well with what we learned by looking over the wall. Women can do more—they already are. Women aren't content to see over the wall. They're climbing the wall. Then they will take the wall down.

It has not been easy. Again, that 10,000 years of programming is tough to overcome. I freak out on what seems to be a regular schedule. I'm not sure if I freak out because she has more crates, or that I don't have enough crates. I always calm down after hours (the whole night, sometimes) of thinking myself back to the difference between equality and equity, between how it's always been and how it needs to be.

Terry is important to me as one symbol of my *anima*—Jung refers to the feminine side of a man as his *anima*. One morning, last year, right before dawn, as if the distant light was building pressure within the darkness which would soon be powerless against it, a photo of Greta Thunberg I'd seen recently flashed in front of me. The photo accompanied an article about young activists who are changing the world.

For me, Greta Thunberg symbolizes the young *anima*. She is young and new. That she is unafraid to speak critically to those in power, is new, is not how women—especially young women—have traditionally acted. And that she speaks with such passion, and emotion, and with some authority which seems to have been granted in deep in the depths of time.

"You are failing us".

"You have stolen my future".

"Shame on you."

Her rise seems fueled not from ego, but by the life force itself. If there are men involved, supporting, influencing, grounding her, they are invisible. In her shadow. Humus.

Her detractors, critics, haters, 'trolls' are mainly establishment Republican pundits. Trump's very condescending tweets to her are not worth repeating. Others, blatantly threatened by this young woman, embarrass themselves in their desperation to diminish anything that might challenge their waning power. I think of the cartoon circulating showing a therapist holding a doll while treating an angry white man. The Caption: "Now show me on this doll where Greta Thunberg has hurt you." This scenario could not be more simple or more obvious: *The decaying white masculine being replaced by the new feminine will be the story of our time. We are watching the feminization of power.*

Another photo appeared to me that same week. It was taken during the U.N. Climate Conference. The photographer, Andrew Hofstetter of Reuters, focused his camera on Greta Thunberg as she watched Trump move through the room. Hofstetter catches the slightly blurred Trump just before he passes between Thunberg and the camera. Greta Thunberg does not appear angry or sad. If a look be both contemplative and decisive at once, this look was. The look on Greta Thunberg's face also tells the story of an immortal and fierce commitment. The 'Trump' she watches is not the leader of the free world, or the embodiment of climate change denial, but one obstacle whose power is no match for her own.

Rather than move out of Terry's shadow, I will stay there, realizing it is where my best work is possible, if I'm honest about my role in the future of life. Men everywhere need to move into that shadow, realizing that our time has passed. We also need to make amends for absorbing more than our share of light, and make every possible effort to support, enhance, and love the women who are closest to us, but also those in the distance.

Before Terry and I were married, her grandmother took me aside and said, "Terry is a very old soul."[35] I had a good idea what she meant then and but now understand more about souls, both large and small.

My chair was designed for backpacking. It is lightweight and rolls up into a tube 18 inches long and 4 inches in diameter. Unrolled it is "L" shaped—designed so that I sit on the horizontal section, separated from the ground by its only its thickness, its vertical piece supporting my back. By pulling straps on each side, I can adjust it to "fine-tune my sit angle," according to the catalogue description. 90 degrees seems perfect. It is built to rock with my butt as fulcrum. I'm most comfortable with my back nine inches past vertical, my legs nine inches above horizontal.

Without this chair I would struggle to sit directly on the ground. My knees do not allow me to sit cross-legged on a flat surface. The Lotus, or even semi-lotus meditation positions are out of the question. Traditional meditation is impossible for me as discomfort demands most of my attention. Peter Matthiessen once said that after decades of Buddhist practice and meditation, he wished he'd saved himself the pain and suffering of the proper 'sitting' position and used a chair.

If Earth 'wisdom' is absorbed up through our feet while walking, our 'sit bones' must also be a conduit.

Due either to a force coming up into me as I sit, or from the fire as I stare into it, I feel myself softening. How easily I've looked across the great divide separating Americans and discount anyone over there, assuming that they embrace what have become "Conservative" values: racism, greed, dishonesty, misogyny, and anthropocentrism—the belief that human beings are the most important entity in the universe.

That I see no middle ground may have something to do with not looking for it. Instead, I spend my time piling onto my side of some imaginary scale, reasons like weights hoping to tip it in my direction. I keep piling on weights but the scale I thought mattered, refuses to move.

Getting up from my camp chair requires serious use of my glutes and quads, and then my core. I've now mastered it, able do it in one fluid motion. I wander around getting blood flowing again. Some of the wisdom coming up through my sit bones seems to have pooled and is stagnating in my ass. The wood remaining on my pile seem perfect to last until I leave for home. Grey clouds hang in the high dark sky like art and the air is moist and smells organic.

This scale may not exist. I drop into the familiar angle between the bottom and the back of my chair. Rumi comes to me. A poem I love. I try recalling it: "Between *something* and *something* is a place. I'll meet you there." Of course. I wait for the poem's exact wording to come to me, but I have what I need: no static scale, no place to go meet halfway between me and them—too far for either of us. But because of Rumi, "beyond" not "between".

Staring into the fire, Rumi's words appear,

"Beyond rightdoing and wrongdoing
There is a field.
I'll meet you there."

And later in the poem, *"don't go back to sleep"*.

Sitting there the poem evolves, shifts, becomes

Beyond **right** *doing and* **left** *doing*
There is a field.
I'll meet you there.

"Beyond."

"Between" does not appear in either the poem's original or evolved form. If a point exists 'between' the left and the right—in the 'middle'—it is too far for either to move. "Beyond" suggests a different dimension, a new possibility.

For my purposes, Rumi refers to idea that those I consider *wrong*, not only think they're *right*, but think that I'm wrong. Hence the scale we've created to measure who is the *most right*.

For me, as it was for Aldo Leopold, "A **thing is right** *when it tends to preserve the integrity, stability, and beauty of the biotic community. It is wrong when it tends otherwise.*"

Clearly, both the fire and the wisdom coming up from the ground tell me that yes, *there is a field* beyond where we are. I'm certain it is a wild field, where the "biotic community" functions according to its evolution, in its 'integrity, stability, and beauty."

I know that field. Yet in all my earnestness, eagerness, and ego, no one from the other side would want, in a thousand years, to meet me there.

If yesterday I'd been asked how I might contribute to healing—rather than increasing—the divide existing in America, I would have said, "healing is impossible, the divide too wide."

I feel differently. Perhaps the divide is too great, too far to reach across. *But in the distance, **beyond**, out there in the future, might be a place to meet.* A wild place. I don't need to 'reach over the divide'. My role is to keep probing wildness not for answers but ideas, possibilities, and articulate what I've found in a form that might inspire someone from across the great divide to meet me there.

A tall order, I think, and then as a small twig explodes into flame.

Integrity. Stability. Beauty.

Beyond, not between.

A wild place. Where this change is possible. No! Where change is constant.

Any wild place.

Sitting in that field.

Stay awake.

The air stills and the grey sky drops, closing in around me. The sun is a faded yellow ball hanging over my shoulder. My shrinking world is now so small that I can touch its edges with my hands, its center lit by fire. Time stops, nothing moves, even the flames are stranded mid-flicker. I wait motionless.

A gap opens in the center of the fire and time gasps and then oozes out from the flame. The present first and then the past in perfect order, carried up on rising smoke.

In four years, using imperceptible breezes time covered my previous presence with fine red sand, one burned bone-shaped branch and a handful of charcoal, the only evidence of who I was. Everything else recovered.

In the smoke, history and horse-drawn wagons move between these canyons. Prehistory follows, flowing up through this fire. Ancient ones squat around here in the darkness, waiting for hunting light. Between history and pre-history, money replaces magic and the spirits leave as the trees they've inhabited forever are cut and sold, when their stones are smashed, and the earth cut open and planted. Some of us lose our color, somehow making us special and entitled to all and anything we can take, using any force available to us.

Then, in the orange center of the flame our consciousness splits as we sense *of our own existence*, separating us from all other life. We become distinct.

Weather and floods and the quaking of the earth, cracks form, slabs fall, all of it. We set this first fire to watch and cook over a million years ago, not here (but maybe here) but there, far away. Our ancestors, but one species among many all pushed forward into the future in the flow of evolution.

From somewhere deep beneath the middle of the fire, Dinosaurs rise and wander the land, 200 million years ago. Some left tracks still visible in the Entrada Sandstone, a few miles away. Tides of shallow seas wash across the landscape, leaving mud and burying a billion creatures. Time presses these ancient seas to limestone and siltstone, some filled with the carbon which burned, now fuels our economy and destroys our climate. Wind moves sand into different layers, one on top of another, forming massive many-colored walls of different hardness and depth. Continents form and drift.

Different climates baked and cooled the earth. The middle of my fire becomes a steamy swamp where life first rises from what was dust of exploding stars.

Then, finally, in the fire's center only darkness speckled with tiny particles the color of possibility.

The passing of all the time on earth seems to have taken no time, if the amount of wood consumed is any indication—none, as nearly as I can tell. A small stack still needs burning and the water remaining in my pot needs to be converted to tea.

One stick I will not burn—the arm-stick from my previous trip. Holding it, turning it around, I recalled finding it yesterday, feeling a rush of something. Not air. Certainly energy of some kind. The energy of memory, the stories created in that spot four years earlier, but more. 'Sacred' is the only word I had to describe what this site has become. Saying that word feels presumptuous.

A place is sacred if it is the site of a transformative event or events—stories or songs or hell, a battle for that matter; death or many deaths. Of some form of consecration—made sacred by a holy person with the power to do so. My native European ancestors had 'sacred' trees and standing stones, and springs. Mountains which were different from other mountains. These features had *genius loci* (spirit of place) and *anima loci* ("place-soul") because of the stories told and the songs sung about them across the ages. Modernism made these relationships obsolete when we chose price over value, resource over source, and personal power over deep collective meaning.

The idea of 'sacred', I believe, is something that in modern life, we have pushed out to the farthest border of what we consider important, and that this is to our peril. "Modernism," notes Nigel Pennick, in his book, *Celtic Sacred Landscapes*,[36] "recognizes no spiritual or even physical difference of note between places". Power and technology obliterated these differences, reducing land "to a random series of virtually uninhabitable 'nowheres', brought into being by denial of place."

Many degrees of "sacred places" must exist. The degree to which a place is 'sacred' may be measured by the numbers who know the story/song/battle/death attached to that site. And over how much time. I may be presumptuous calling a place I've camped twice "sacred". But, it is to me, in the way that the altars we make at home are meaningful to us, and no one else, each of the objects we add, connecting us to a story. A roadside cross is sacred to the family of the person who died there. We don't need to know the story to understand the gesture.

If a week or a year ago someone found my camp and the burnt arm stick, they would not consider this a 'sacred' place. Not without the story.

Over hundreds of years, tens of thousands of Diné, Hopi, Ute Mountain Ute, Hopi, and Zuni people have made pilgrimages to the Bears Ears Region, paying respect to the lands consecrated by their ancestors adds a depth and breadth of 'sacredness' that we Euro-Americans cannot imagine. While our native European ancestors had similar histories with their own consecrated places, we descend from people who for one reason or another cut themselves off from that deep history, forgetting it.

The collective energy of huge numbers of pilgrims with a focused belief imbue a place like Bears Ears with a power which then radiates continually into the present and the future. This might be what "It is time" for. We can begin to learn about this type of power and perhaps through the generosity of our Native brothers and sisters, partake of some of it and feel it for the first time, as the Earth moves into the future, with or without us.

Attaching a powerful personal story to a 'place' makes that place 'sacred'.

"Is Castleton Tower considered 'sacred'"? I wonder hearing the distant voices of climbers above on the tower's North Chimney Route. Evidence exists of ancient hunting parties in Castle Valley. I imagine them at night around their fires. They must have told stories of this magnificent tower, watching over the vast area from above.

Does sound ride on the wind? With the good weather, surely there are many parties attempting to summit, one of America's Fifty Classic Climbs. Only rarely do I hear them calling to each other from various points along the route or talking among themselves at the base. There must be an atmospheric formula determining how well or far sound travels.

Recently it was reported[37] that scientists from the University of Utah had detected a 'pulse' coming from Castleton Tower. This supports what many believe to be true: the Earth is alive. The climbers above me may be 'pilgrims' making a 'pilgrimage' to Castleton, hoping to feel that pulse.

Travelers. Pilgrims. Places. Sacred places.

My visiting my sacred place, makes me a pilgrim.

A pilgrim, not a hermit. Pilgrims need a physical 'sacred place' for pilgrimage. A hermit, at least a 'great' hermit, is a hermit with or without wild deserts or mountains. A hermit is on an inward journey. A pilgrim seeks. A hermit is sought. Hermits travel the universe from wherever they sit.

I'm a seeker.

A sun beam breaks through the clouds which seem darker than before. Wanting a cup of tea, I flicked my lighter a few times unsuccessfully. I just bought it to replace the perfectly good one the rat stole.

God knows why after all those years I chose the day after Trump's 2016 Election to clean that room out. The rat shit and dried cactus, there was no end of horribleness. I've kept it clean ever since. That rat, however, has never left.

He chewed a hole in the bottom of the door which allows him to cruise the library at night pulling right-sized and interesting things into his lair. I've found, over the years a small set of pliers, emitters for the drip system, nuts, bolts, lots of chewed paper. A screwdriver. And my lighter so covered in filth that I threw it away.

Aside from once shorting the electrical power to the water pump, the rat does little actual damage. His main issue is messiness—cactus and pink insulation making up the bulk of it.

I've tried live-trapping him, to no avail—baiting him with pet food (both dog and cat food, wet and dry), peanut butter (smooth and chunky), fruit, chocolate, and cheese (sharp cheddar and parmesan). While sitting on the patio at night, we catch glimpses of him. There on his haunches, his large eyes, we understood why many refer to the *Bushy-tailed Wood Rat* (*Neotoma cinerea*) as "cute."

I found a triple X-sized mouse trap at the local hardware store but had second thoughts about killing the little guy. Instead, I bought a mechanism which when plugged into an electrical outlet, emits a peppermint mist, something rats and mice supposedly hate. I also purchased ($23) peppermint essential oil and a small spray bottle ($1.95) at the Moonflower co-op. I covered the entrance area with peppermint and set the gadget to permanently mist the room's interior.

While the office smelled great, the peppermint did not deter the rat, which came back regularly. What's worse, to mask the peppermint, the rat started bringing dollops of dog shit into the pump room.

A month ago, I was in the hardware store, the 'pest and poison' isle, staring once again at those huge kill traps, contemplating. I realized then how much respect I have for that rat, how hard he works to keep that perfect spot. I actually reached for the trap, but then as if by some miracle, hanging right below it was something I'd not noticed before. An ultrasonic device which emits high-pitched sound pulses, which mice and rats (supposedly) cannot stand. I bought it, took it home, plugged it in.

Three days later, I discovered more dog shit, cactus, and an old polaroid photo of our niece, chewed around the edges. Obviously, the high-pitched sounds had not worked.

Time to kill the little fucker, I thought. At least try to. I'm so sorry.

In the hardware store on my next trip to town, I pulled a large kill trap off its hook surprised by my dispassion.

Back home, I left the rat trap on the counter, still in its package. Later while eating dinner, Terry saw the trap and said, "You're going to kill her? You won't kill anything." I reminded her of just how I'd tried every humane tactic, none successfully. "Just what harm is she causing?" Terry was right. She—I'm referring to the rat as female—had done very little damage.

Terry, as is her role in my life, caused me to re-think my relationship with the rat. In 24 hours, I'd gone from buying a trap, intending to snap her neck to realizing that she hasn't caused much trouble at all, to wonder if, in fact, I'm benefiting from her presence in my life.

While I did not set the kill trap, I kept the sound sounding and the mister misting (although I'd switched from peppermint to oregano oil, as suggested by a neighbor.) When I next checked, what I found astounded me. In addition to a few more shit globules, more cactus, and pink insulation, I found a pipe. Not as in a pipe for plumbing, but a pipe for smoking. A pipe I did not recognize (most of what the rat brings in I know first-hand and have even missed). When I showed Terry the pipe, she said, "she's brought you a peace pipe now that you've decided not to kill her." Of course, that's what's happened.

I'd surely come to some sort of resolution with the rat. Hmmm, weird that I almost wrote "solution with the rat," and how close those two words are. How can a re-solution be the do-over or the re-doing of a solution? I've not previously 'solved' the problem that rat is causing me. I looked up "resolve," the verb, and found that it means to "settle or come to a solution." The "to settle" part sounds right. To me, a 'solution' is 'active,' where "re-solve" implies passivity, which is the case with the rat and me.

My lighter finally ignites, and the stove hums, and I wait in the still air for the water to boil, the storm still hours away. I'll sip my tea, watching fire turn the last sticks to ash.

Kneeling, I lean over my dead fire and pull sand across it, covering the smoking embers, which I soak with the last of my water. The popping and sizzles I hear come from the center of the Earth.

I'll soon be home and know the election results. As it often has, my mind defaults to those four possible scenarios[38] that made sense to me and comforted me four years ago. Only the fourth scenario remains: "Trump- runs again and god forbid—wins, and we wait four more years." I catch myself. I shudder knowing that the implications embedded in the reality of the fourth scenario are of a different dimension now than then. Questions of what these past four years have really meant to our country, but more—to the future of our species are more than I can comprehend. In particular, the phrase, "….we wait four more years," stands out. Wait for what? I ask out loud. For things to return to normal? What? When 'normal' is crazy? Which is what I referred to then. But now? Normal is devastating. Hopefully, 'normal' is yet another victim of the Hermit Virus. I breathe deeply knowing that based on what we've seen and heard and experienced, that the fourth scenario has changed to "depending on the outcome of the election either we continue accelerating along the short cut to our own extinction, or we delay it, slowing it down, and hopefully, find a transition to a sounder path".

Years earlier, in MBA school, we'd spent days debated the question: *Can the current system be fixed, or do we take it down and start over.* Then, I'd been on the side of the fixable system. Over the years, I have changed. Trump cinched it. If 'the system' can accommodate someone like him, it needs to be replaced. But Biden represents the traditional system. If he becomes the next president, his goal will be repairing the damage done—slowing down our inevitable end but not changing it. If Trump wins again, he will surely complete his destruction of the system. My commitment is soft, I think, taking another sip of tea. That I pray for Biden's victory means I am fine with the current, tattered system. Yes, the system needs to come down. But after I'm gone.

I sit, hoping for any excuse not to get moving. Finding none, I twist, flex and rise from my chair quite gracefully, I think. I pack rhythmically and finish by rolling up my chair then strap it to the top of my full pack. The wind rises all around me. I check my fire for the last time and finding it cool, I pull the few remaining charcoal chunks and put them in my small baggie of trash which goes in a side pocket of my pack. I spread the pow-ered ash—all that remains of my fire—in a small circle to be blown off by the wind. Next time, I will find no sign of having been here before.

Without the water and food, my pack becomes an invisible part of me. I survey my camp one last time for any 'micro trash' then turn and drop off my perch toward the trail. I feel strong and happy and so loose that I just stand there while the path toward the pass flows beneath me.

The path is well worn from many hikers moving along it in both directions. It climbs at a gradual, nearly unnoticeable angle, only steepening in three places where it crosses small canyons.

I follow the path as it clings to the northwest side of the canyon, which slopes away from the Wingate Sandstone into which weather and time have carved Castleton Tower, the Priest, and Nuns. I pass through the Cutler Formation, which blends into the Moenkopi, which slopes toward the Kayenta, atop which sits the radical Wingate cliffs. The path curves to the right and rises up onto a nearly horizontal gray rim, its steep side dropping away to my left. A dozen minor canyons cut up the terrain below me. A bright force forces itself up the main washes, looking for weak points in the landscape to fill as it branches and branches again nearly to the rim, all at the speed of light, crackling as it goes. I hurry, hoping not to be caught.

The pass comes into view, its shadow a dark contrast to the grey clouds beyond. The sun, even weakened to an impotent yellow orb by the gauzy sky, holds unknown promise.

With some trepidation, I climb the last hundred meters to the pass. I turn and watch as churning clouds fill in behind me, hiding my camp until next time.

Across the valley, the weight of the thick grey sky pins the last sunbeams against the edge of Porcupine Rim. This compresses them into four giant lasers of light burning deep into the nearby cliffs, which then give off an orange glow. Rain streaks the southern sky with a beauty that dissolves any threat.

The storm rises up behind me, pushing dust into clouds ahead of it. The wind is warm, and strong, and constant.

Not eager to finish my walk, I take off my pack and sit down in the soft sand against a boulder that forms a shield against the oncoming storm. The giant Mary Jane Wilderness spreads out behind me, and beyond, Fisher Towers, which, blending into the cliff from which they were formed, are only visible by their shadows. Castle Valley rises up in front of me, and the storm blows behind me. A pair of ravens call out as they swoop across the great distance. Dressed in black, they become figure skaters without skates, without the hard, cold limiting dimension of ice. They twirl and tumble, slicing sensuous curves into the clouds. I can't see it, but I know where our house is, two miles away. Unconsciously, I gauge the wind speed, the light, the cloud cover to know when I must leave to beat the storm.

From here, I know the way. Not a trail really, but a 'way'—a familiar path which may have footprints, but often does not— toward the giant boulders, the Cave that is No Longer a Cave, carved into the largest of them. The path passes between the boulders along a dry creek, defined by how recently water has flowed through it. It will then turn left along the high edge of the wash into which I will drop just before passing the beneath the old barbed wire, stretched head-high across the wash, which has recently deepened into a 'gulch.' The gulch curves at the huge Juniper, half of its roots exposed by a flood, and now it hangs suspended, only half of it still living. Then the gulch intersects the main dirt road connecting the canyons. I will follow this half a mile to the Portal, through which I will pass, physically, emotionally, and spiritually. On the other side I will meet modern life and ordinary reality exactly where I left it.

From here, I know the way.

I love sitting but feel drawn into the invisible flow that will take me down and back across the flats, Middle World, home. I imagine how migrating sandhill cranes feel because this is how I feel, that I've ridden the thermals high, to this point, now ready to glide and wait for the next thermal, which I will ride home.

I've worried that my "one story" was wrong. That I've kept following it and telling it because I was too old and had invested too much into it. Perhaps my story is fine but too short. The length of the past on which I've based my story is too short, as is the future. My story begins in the Pleistocene, with my earliest ancestors, *Homo sapien*. But this is *not* the beginning of the story. In the context of the complete story, "my" story, the one I tell over and over again, is only a fragment. I will lengthen my story, watch it travel down the far twigs into the branches of the Tree of Life, then into its trunk. Into its roots where the first life first throbbed then moved in that perfect pond. But then, what about the stardust and the stars which exploded into that dust? And before that?

Extending my past, according to my theory, also extends my future. Except, *what if*— that phrase again—what I see looking back past any logical beginning is the same view looking into the future beyond any logical end? No beginning and no end. The *beginning* is not the beginning, but the end of the end, which is the new beginning.

That there might be no beginning and no actual end I cannot quite get my head around.

"*What a relief…nothing is born*", wrote Red Pine when he signed his translation of Yung Chia's "Song of Enlightenment" for me as a gift.[39] I had no clue what he meant, then, and only glimmers now. One of the poem's lines is, "to be truly not born is to be not not born."

But then another, "the acceptance that nothing arises or is born is the final attainment prior to enlightenment," which comforts me.

And "When you can't find it, that's when you'll find it" *How far do I look and not find it before I find it?*

The next four years and the four after that....

A lot could have happened in the short time I've been gone. Or nothing. Perhaps time has slowed for the entire planet as it has for me. Or stopped.

I don't care. Of course, I 'care', but I'm less willing to let the outcome of an election affect me. Why?

Anxious for context, I've been reading more history. Modern America has a fairly recent history. We know this but forget. Most other countries have suffered through authoritarian despotic leaders and have survived, albeit not without suffering. China, for example, has gone through many changes in dynasty, many of them accompanied by mass death and insufferable longing. Why would America be immune?

Trump's role for me has been to expose America's dark, draconian, racist, misogynist, violent, mostly white, mostly male underbelly, which has not, as I'd assumed, disappeared but has been simmering beneath the surface. Now, we are being held to account. We can see it. I've faced reality if our leaders have no ethics, our laws simply will not work. America can be a brutal country. It can also be a beautiful one. Above all, it is complicated and paradoxical. Regardless of how sophisticated we become, how many of life's mysteries we are able to quantify and explain, the rules of the Tao will continue applying to us, just as they do to everything that lives, has lived, or will live. "Too far this way or that, and extinction risk grows."

I believe the world's indigenous leaders who claim that *It is time*. Our next president will not—cannot—change this.

Whoever our next president is, I hope to move on through my life with love, not hate—with joy and trust in the collective good, knowing that one's true self is evolutionary and the continual search for it is the seed of happiness. I will remember what these rocks have taught me about time: our small, short lifetimes juxtaposed against and contained within the background of immense, endearing time, enduring, evolutionary time during which the universe continually reveals itself in the wildness that can be found wherever it is sought. I will always be seeking wildness: the pilgrim *and* the hermit exploring both the outer *and* inner wilderness. The Way. Wildness is the way—the Tao.

And what if the Tao is at the root of that idea that those early monks, living in wildness, in their contemplative solitude, contributed non-locally—"action at a distance"—to a better world? Lived well—consciously, contemplatively, joyously— our lives have that same potential.

The dropping light sucks me so deeply into the present moment I consider not moving—ever again. Just watching. Just being. Not going home. The hum of the ten thousand things generating, constant, alive, is as loud as the consistent breeze bringing the storm, becoming a song.

The choice to sit or move on dissolves, and I stand up and swing my pack onto my shoulders, assuming that I have what I've come for. From here, the way is familiar.

The first raindrops plink behind me, then onto my pack, and then I feel them on my head. The shifting wind forces me to re-balance. I stop in front of the "Cave that is no longer a Cave" and bow. Although I've been here fifteen times—not counting the dozens of shamanic journeys, I've never seen what I see now.

A Pleistocene bison has just moved up from the valley into the storm, a mighty boulder carved by the wind. Its massive head faces the adjacent slope it is about to climb into the oncoming gale. Wilma Mankiller, Chief the Cherokee said, "Cows run away from the storm while the buffalo charges toward it— and gets through it quicker. Whenever I'm confronted with a tough challenge, I do not prolong the torment. I become the buffalo".

The stone bison's shoulders rise above his short neck into its give-away hump. Its back slopes away from its hump and then curves down its perfect haunches. This bison did not exist when the cave was still a cave. Sometime after my 2016 trip, rain filled the dry streambed, flushing away the dirt that had formed the cave's back. The bison's sloping underbelly was created when water flowed beneath it, exposing what have become the legs on which the bison now stands.

Either I'd never stopped to look at that boulder from that angle, or I'd never needed to see it until now. Perhaps the bison has just appeared. (Terry took this photo a few days later.)

The wind strengthens, pushing me home ahead of the storm. Large drops pit the dry earth like bullets being shot from the clouds, and because dancing is the only way to dodge them, I dance. I dance with the leaves and dust swirling in the wind and with the wind itself moving down the canyon.

EPILOGUE

I WILL STEP THROUGH THE PORTAL into air that is fresh but more. It will be new air, washed-clean air. Washed by wind and rain and wind again, and then dried by the sun, the light from which engulfed the entire valley. I will feel heat that I've never felt, not quantity but quality, deep and rich. Heat I will store and draw from when needed.

Biden will be the President-Elect. Trump will not go peacefully, insisting that the election was stolen from him while raising millions of dollars in support of "The Big Lie." He will incite an 'insurrection' of thousands of his (mainly) white, (mainly) male followers to overwhelm the United States Capital in an attempt to interrupt the official and ceremonial count of the electoral votes, while threatening the lives of our leaders, including Vice President Michael Pence. People will die. Biden will take the oath of office. We will be stunned by a young African American woman reciting the inaugural poem. We will breathe easier, momentarily. Trump will be impeached for a second time. With support from Republicans—many whose lives were threatened by the riots Trump encouraged—he will once again be acquitted. Still, we will sleep as we've not slept for years. We will work hard and hope that President Biden and Vice President Harris will be required to reweave the tattered fabric of democracy while attempting to heal the divides. We will see that the 'story' of Trump does not end with his presidency because it is not the 'story of Trump,' but the story of what the Spore has done to the minds of Republican leaders, going back decades. The 'story' will not end because the factors in place that led to Trump, that allowed an arrogant reality tv personality to be our President, are still in place: the political-economic system based on White supremacy, promising to free us from our evolutionary responsibilities, quickening the demise of our species; the republicans who will, if necessary, sacrifice democracy for power and seek to change election laws to hang onto what little of that power remains.

Why should we be immune?

I will look back at the 'bullet' we dodged and see that where we are headed, a bit slower now with a reasonable person as a leader, is still toward our own extinction. I will ask myself repeatedly if our brain, the brain we used to both create the technologies that have quickened our demise and predict our own demise, might also be the brain that can save us. But then, the last (of many) grand mistakes will be ignoring what we 'know' while letting politics cripple us. The "ten thousand things" will generate perpetually. Vaccines will slow the spread of the Hermit Virus. The economy will stop choking and gasping, and we will hear a distant humming with the passage of an economic aid package. More of our tax money will once again be spent helping one another rather than benefiting the wealthy. A young male white supremacist/evangelical Christian "having a bad day" will murder eight people, six of them Asian-American women, in three Asian-owned businesses. Trump will continue as the head of the Republican party, which like some strange fish, will completely rot before it dies.

Deb Haaland will wear turquoise dragonfly earrings, traditional moccasins, and skirt embroidered with corn and butterflies to be sworn in as Secretary of the Interior. She will be the first Native American cabinet member, becoming the conduit through which Indigenous Knowledge will pass to American culture, which desperately needs it. Early one morning, I will look out across Middle World, over the pass, to the shadowed cliffs forming the eastern edge of Mary Jane Canyon and watch light pooled on the rim by the rising sun cascade down the stone's longest edge.

After discovering that she had destroyed the insulation near the engine of our car, and chewed through the wiring, dismantling our irrigation system, I will finally and regrettably kill the rat. With the large trap baited with very expensive almond butter. Her absence is presence.

On a nearly-spring day in March, exactly one year since the official beginning of the Hermit Virus, we will meet our friend, Lauren, at the river. Calder, her 2-year-old son, will be with her. Calder and I will build a small fire and throw rocks into the river. On that day, all my questions will have answers: are there spiders? How much does an invisible fish weigh? Will the flat stone sink or skip once it hits the river? After discovering that she had destroyed the insulation near the engine of our car, and chewed through the wiring, dismantling our irrigation system, I will finally and regrettably kill the rat. With the large trap baited with very expensive almond butter. Her absence is presence.

We will continue wearing a mask, which works for both the Hermit Virus and the Spore, but only if it covers the nose as well as the mouth.

ENDNOTES

[1] This is part of the story my mentor and friend Bill Kittredge helped me "find". He'd said that his goal as a teacher was to "help his students find the one story that they will tell over and over the rest of their lives." At first this seemed boring but later I realized it was true.

[2] *Tools for Grassroots Activists*, Gallagher and Meyers; Patagonia, 2016 (3rd Edition) page 203.

[3] Over a month later on Dec. 28, President Obama proclaimed Bears Ears National Monument.

[4] "*This Moment: Erosion of Democracy*", Erosion, By Terry Tempest Williams, Picador, 2020.

[5] Exhausted at the end of that December day we moved into Castle Valley, I'd found a lawn chair and sat down in it in the sun. I couldn't believe that the move was done and that we'd be sleeping in our new home. I dozed off as the shadow crossed the valley. As it covered me, the air temperature dropped I swear 40 degrees so fast that I feared I would not be able to get out of the chair before freezing to death. Never again.

[6] This from an essay I wrote for *The Brooklyn Rail*, "Walking, Foot as Conduit". March, 2020

[7] Much has been written about the women of the far right. Plus, deep history suggests that a massive population explosion occurred with the advent of agriculture, when women, no longer required to find food, could have more than one baby at her breast at one time. Could this have been when men took power from women? See Helen Fisher, *The Anatomy of Love*. W.W. Norton Co. 2016

[8] "The Latin term *sacrificium* (a sacrifice) derived from Latin *sacrificus* (performing priestly functions or sacrifices), which combined the concepts *sacra* (sacred things) and *facere* (to do or perform)."

[9] *Spiritual Tourism: Travel and Religious Practice in Western Society*, by Alex Norman; Continuum, 2011

[10] Hawken, Paul (2007). *Blessed Unrest: How the Largest Movement in the World Came into Being and Why No One Saw It Coming*. New York: Viking.

[11] "*Christianity split the Germanic barbarian into an upper and a lower half, and enabled him, by repressing the dark side, to domesticate the brighter half and fit it for civilization. But the lower, darker half still awaits redemption and a second spell of domestication. Until then, it will remain associated with the vestiges of the prehistoric age, with the collective unconscious, which is subject to a peculiar and ever-increasing activation. As the Christian view of the world loses its authority, the more menacingly will the "blond beast" be heard prowling about in its underground prison, ready at any moment to burst out with devastating consequences. When this happens in the individual it brings about a psychological revolution, but it can also take a social form.*" C.G. Jung; Collected Works, Vol. 10, paragraph 17; Bollingen Series, 1964.

[12] "We live in bodies that are relatively unchanged since the Pleistocene and yet we're trying to make them work in a world vastly different from that for which evolution designed them. This may be at the root of many problems we face."

[13] *Climate Change has Helped Fuel a Megadrought in the Southwest*; Chelsea Harvey, E & E News, April 17, 2020.

[14] According to Justin McBrien in his recent article in *Truthout*, "in the midst of the First Extermination Event"—extermination by capitalism.

[15] Mcmullin garnered a respectable 21.54% of the Utah vote.

[16] Taoism's "The Way"—Explained by Evolutionary Biology. By Sol, *Medium*, Sept. 28, 2019

[17] The Tao of Physics. 25th Anniversary Edition, Fritjof Capra, Shambala, 2000. Page 25.

[18] "Are Utah's Politicians Evil", by Brooke Williams, Medium, Dec. 19, 2017.

[19] See *American Mania*. Peter Whybrow, W. W. Norton & Company; 1st edition (January 17, 2005)

[20] the Jewish theologian, Abraham Joshua Heschel. Turns out that this brilliant, twentieth century American rabbi had much to say about 'awe'. "Wisdom", he said, "is fostered by awe". That [awe] is the *root* of faith, that awe must guide us. We 'avoid' insight when we lose awe. "Forfeit your sense of awe....and the world becomes a marketplace for you." "Awe", he said, "is more than an emotion; it is a way of understanding, insight into a meaning greater than ourselves.

[21] "A life of solitude and labour, poverty and fasting, charity and prayer which enabled the old superficial self to be purged away and permitted the gradual emergence of the true secret self in which the Believer and Christ were 'one spirit." *Wisdom of the Desert*, Thomas Merton; New Directions Paperback, 1970.

[22] *Wild Identity*, White Fish Review, Sept, 2020.

[23] *Cheddar Man,* "What Kind of Ancestor Do You Want to Be?" University of Chicago Press, 2021.

[24] *Illustrating "Equality" vs. "Equity",* Interaction Institute; January, 2016

[25] From *Song of the Open Road,* by Walt Whitman

[26]http://online.sfsu.edu/rone/buddhism/yogacara/transformation%20of%20consciousness.htm

[27]Richard Berret, *What My Soul Told Me*

[28] Survival, which is about never having enough and not trusting the universe to provide for them. They must stay vigilant about watching their money, which, I believe, includes expending huge effort to be sure that no one takes theirs, even the government who is surely giving it away to those less worthy. Relationship conscious people are those who may not have received the love an affection they needed in childhood, and remain focused on belonging throughout their lives. I've often wondered if many of Trump's MAGA hat-wearing supporters are more attracted to the idea of belonging to a large group, than they are to what that group actually stands for. No matter how much praise and acknowledgment they get, those of "Self-Esteem Consciousness' always need more. They seek power for the sake of power, as an ends regardless of the means it requires. They want acknowledgment from those with more power, regardless of who they are or what they stand for.

[29] Duality comes up frequently while reading Red Pine's small chat book, his translations of the fifteen-hundred year old, *Trusting the Mind: Zen Epigrams* by Seng Ts'an. Empty Bowl Press, 2019

[30] From Wikipedia: "**Bread and circuses**" (or **bread and games**; from Latin: *panem et circenses*) is a metonymic phrase referring to superficial appeasement. It is attributed to Juvenal, a Roman poet active in the late first and early second century CE — and is used commonly in cultural, particularly political, contexts.

In a political context, the phrase means to generate public approval, not by excellence in public service or public policy, but by diversion, distraction or by satisfying the most immediate or base requirements of a populace[1] — by offering a palliative: for example food (bread) or entertainment (circuses)."

[31] My early book, *Halflives: Reconciling Work and Wildness*. Island Press; 1999.

[32] "Franco Battiato was asked what he thought of those ascetics who retire from the world to live in solitude and meditation, an attitude that at first seems to lead to an escape from the world more than a commitment in favour of an improvement. The famous singer told the interviewer that one could not even imagine how good those people did for humanity with their attitude of «apparent» escape. With the theory of morphic fields in fact the Battiato's thesis is easily explainable and understandable: if the ascetic achieves a high degree of spiritual development, through morphic resonance, synchronously the other members of his species would be affected - even if unconsciously of course - as the change goes to affect the unconscious rather than the conscious... 'Changing the world by changing ourselves', a well-known esoteric truth seem to echo here."

From *On the Concept of Synchronicity: Jung between Psychoanalysis and Quantism*; Lucio Giuliodori; Create Space, Independent Publishing Platform, 2015.

[33] "The Self-Aware Universe" Amit Goswami, Putnam; 1993. Page 76

[34] *Why Two Chefs in Small Town Utah are Battling President Trump*; New Yorker Magazine, Katherine Schulz, Oct. 1, 2018.

[35]Mimi meant it in relation to re-incarnation, but not exactly--that our souls are continually being birthed into new lives, with new test and growth opportunities. "Old souls" have been through more cycles of this than young souls and are wiser as a result.

[36]"Celtic Sacred Landscapes", Pennick, Nigel. Thames & Hudson; 1st Edition (March 1, 1996)

[37]*The Resonance of Stone*, in Erosion, by Terry Tempest Williams, 2019.

[38] 1) that Trump's crimes would catch up with him and he'd either resign or be impeached; 2) that he would continue to be himself, do a terrible job, announce that he would not seek re-election; 3) He would seek reelection with the support of a group of crazy republicans. Other Republicans would back a more reasonable candidate, defeating Trump in the primary. 4) He runs again and is re-elected.

[39] *The Song of Enlightenment*, by Yung-chia Hsuan-chuch (665(?)-713) remains one of the most popular Zen texts in East Asia.

ACKNOWLEDGMENTS

I acknowledge that this place is traditional territory of the Núu-agha-tūvū-pū (Ute) people, whose current presence and influence I feel. I also acknowledge that most place names represent only the most recent human history of colonizing and settling the west, a history in which my own ancestors played a destructive role.

Leslie M. Browning, at Homebound Press, provided calm but firm guidance throughout the creation of this book, and with Gail Steeves Collins-Ranadive chose me as one runner up for the Prism Prize, from which this book springs.

Anne Backer and Jane Watkins are a constant source of support and encouragement.

For their stewardship, inspiration, and friendship, Peter Lawson and Anne Wilson are implacable.

Lynne Tempest, Sarah Hedden, and Andy Nettell read the earliest versions, becoming lodestars along the way.

Parts of this book were originally published in White Fish Review ("Metamorphosis" 2021) and "What Kind of Ancestor Do You Want to Be?" (University of Chicago Press, 2021) in different form.

Thank you, Philip Graves, for the cover photo, Terry Tempest Williams for the photo of the bison boulder and me, and Gloria Sanchez for the Hermit Tarot Card on the back page. Thank you, Leslie M. Browning for the book's design, both inside and out.

Red Pine and David Hinton, wise and gentle guides, helped me past difficult obstacles while I searched for essential truths.

Terry Tempest Williams, who spent whole days helping me on this specific project, has been my foundation, inspiration, and muse for nearly half a century. Who I would be without her is neither acceptable nor recognizable.

ABOUT THE AUTHOR

Brooke Williams writes about evolution, consciousness, and his own adventures exploring both the inner and outer wilderness. He believes that the length of the past equals the length of the future. He lives with the writer, Terry Tempest Williams near Moab, Utah, where they watch light and wait for rain.

HOMEBOUND
PUBLICATIONS

We are an award-winning independent publisher founded in 2011 striving to ensure that the mainstream is not the only stream. More than a company, we are a community of writers and readers exploring the larger questions we face as a global village. It is our intention to preserve contemplative storytelling. We publish full-length introspective works of creative non-fiction, literary fiction, and poetry. *Fly with us into our 10th year.*

WWW.HOMEBOUNDPUBLICATIONS.COM

CPSIA information can be obtained
at www.ICGtesting.com
Printed in the USA
JSHW020858291221
21619JS00005B/5